METAMORPHOSIS THROUGH THE

OMEGA

DIMENSION

milena

M PUBLISHING

Illustrations
Zorica and Dragan Jovanović Ignjatov
zodrag@gmail.com

Copy-Editing
Rick Mughal
galactronix@hotmail.com

Publisher
M PUBLISHING

Printed by
Lightning Source, United Kingdom

A catalogue record for this book is
available from the British Library

ISBN
978-1-909323-01-8

CONTENTS

RUMI

In May of 2000, at a spiritual conference in London, I picked up a glossy magazine entirely compiled of excerpts from the *Knowledge Book*. The title of the magazine, printed by the *World Brotherhood Union Mevlana Supreme Foundation* in Istanbul, was *Millennium Magazine*. When I opened it and started to read, I could not stop. It felt like the information in those words was what I had always been looking for.

Some rare sense of self-reassurance emerged from this experience and I immediately knew I wanted to read the whole book. So, I ordered the *Knowledge Book* from the Foundation in Istanbul and it arrived on the 21st of June - Summer Solstice, and the only day in the year when the Omega dimension is directly open to our planet!

I took the parcel to my desk, unpacked it, and the purple-gold book lay in front of me. After savouring its unique visual beauty, I opened it at random and my eyes rested on the word *Rumi*. I closed the book, puzzled by finding a reference to Rumi, and then I opened it again. This time it was a few hundred pages further on. My eyes focused on a line and, again, the first word I noticed was *Rumi!*

Back then, I had been reading Rumi's poetry every night for years. The energy of his writing was soothing to my entire being. It would take me to an inner place of peace and love, helping me to go through the reality of the war that was happening in my mother country, the typical challenges of an immigrant, financial uncertainties and the like.

Whoever brought me here, will have to take me home.

Mevlana Celaleddin-i Rumi

NEW BIRTH

I did not expect to find Rumi mentioned in the *Knowledge Book*. Even more unexpected was to find him in the two consecutive random openings of the book – particularly after I later discovered that within 1111 pages of the entire book, Rumi was mentioned only a few times. So, while processing what had just happened in my first encounter with the purple-gold book, I slowly closed it and the only way I could express my feelings was to scream loudly… and I did!

The scream came as a spontaneous reaction to a multidimensional alignment that suddenly demonstrated itself to me. With it I embraced all the experiences, which had been leading me to that moment, and felt an instinctive gratitude for encountering the *Knowledge Book*. Overwhelmed with these impressions, I was both excited and relieved – as if an aeons-old appointment had finally taken place.

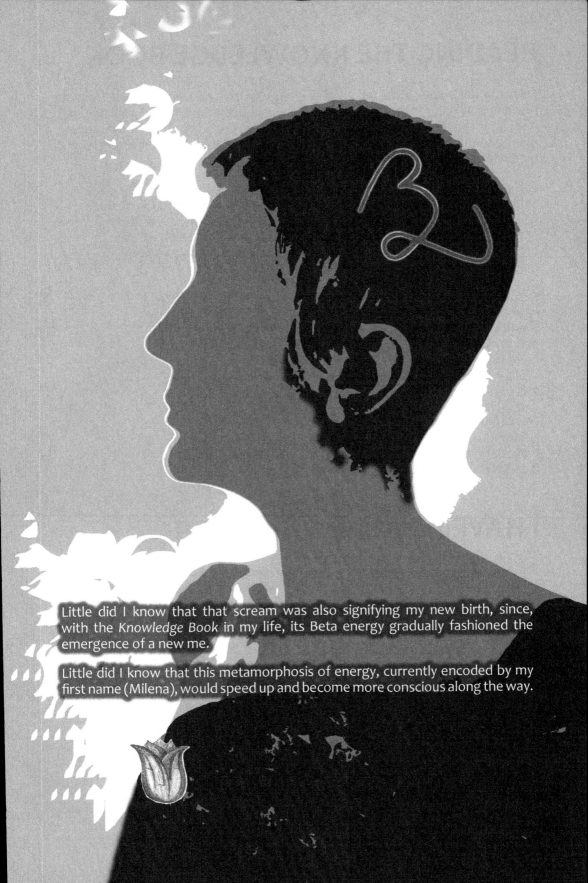

Little did I know that that scream was also signifying my new birth, since, with the *Knowledge Book* in my life, its Beta energy gradually fashioned the emergence of a new me.

Little did I know that this metamorphosis of energy, currently encoded by my first name (Milena), would speed up and become more conscious along the way.

READING THE KNOWLEDGE BOOK

Even though I was attracted to the energy of the *Knowledge Book* from the beginning, it did not mean I was able to fully understand what I was reading. Also, I noticed that the linguistic aspect of the book was unusual. The formation of long sentences is uncommon, as well as the liberal use of capital letters with no obvious patterns behind their placement.

The reasons for not fully understanding the text of the *Knowledge Book* could be many. One such reason comes from the fact that much of the information in the book is to be accessed in the future, when a particular energy intensity with a corresponding consciousness level will be present on the planet. Until then, some sentences, paragraphs or messages cannot be fully grasped.

Despite these unusual characteristics of the *Knowledge Book*, I have been reading and enjoying it ever since. I have noticed how the book facilitates a broadening of my view-point on the Self and on Creation. I have also noticed how the book makes me more positive while it steadily unfolds a better human in me. It facilitates progressive change evident in all those who read it, and that is an extraordinary power of the *Knowledge Book*.

Due to its inherent cosmic techniques, the book conveys cosmic light and unlocks our Godly Essence. It gradually unveils our essential virtues and introduces us to our real selves – hence it is called the *Book of Essence*.

I HAVE BECOME STRONGER

The very experience of reading the *Knowledge Book*, and applying the programmes related to it, has awakened in me the memory of my cosmic roots. It has shed light on the cause-and-effect chain of cosmic affairs that I am a part of. In equal measure, the book has given me the answers relevant to my purpose for being here and now on this planet.

The book has also opened a new door to my inner being and with every passing day takes me closer to my *Essence*[1], where the universal truth of who I am is coded. It offers me a context for life in which everything is more meaningful and acceptable. As a result, I have become stronger: mentally, emotionally and even physically. How have I noticed that?

It has become easier for me to accept all that I go through in my life. This does not mean that before I met the *Knowledge Book* I was lacking spiritual understanding of the importance of accepting and aligning with the Will of God – even religious books were teaching us that.

The strength, I am talking about, has come as a conscious ability to supervise and control myself better through the many challenges that still exist. This new capacity, reflected in my behaviour, has clearly resulted from the energetic benefits of working with this cosmic book.

These positive physical changes were most evident after I completed the programme of writing the *Knowledge Book* in my own handwriting. Some energy work was done on my lower chakras while I was writing, undoing some blockages I was not even aware of, and as a result my body returned to its state of lightness I remembered having only in my twenties.

Through my engagement with the programmes of the *Knowledge Book*, I have been witnessing an ample supply of energy, as well as a continuous boost of motivation for philanthropic efforts. Also, I am able to observe how the time it takes me to process information, make decisions and to act upon these decisions is becoming shorter, while my confidence and joy steadily grow. It is becoming apparent to me that the lower the energies we dwell upon, the less ability we have to take control of our body and our thoughts, words and actions.

How do we make up for our evolutionary energy deficiencies?

With the use of cosmic techniques unknown to modern science, and as a direct book of the Lord[2], the *Knowledge Book* has been prepared to most efficiently facilitate that very process and to unfold the *perfect human being*[3] in us. It makes us stronger in many ways, helping us to face and transcend our remaining weaknesses.

Therefore, in relation to overcoming evolutionary challenges, the path of the *Knowledge Book* may be considered the definitive option.

NEW DEFINITIONS

After more than ten years with the *Knowledge Book* in my life, my understanding of reality, of truth, and of who I am is still noticeably growing under its light. Equally so, my amazement with the book expands literally every single day.

On this planet, we currently do not possess an adequate enough word to apply to the phenomenon that is the *Knowledge Book*, except for the word *book*. Yet the *Knowledge Book* is far more than that, for it is able to scan the evolutionary level of the person who reads it and to energetically adjust to each reader. At the same time, the book changes its own aura in response to the *cosmic energy*[4] continuously arriving on Earth, and reflects the actual cosmic energy present at the moment of reading.

Since, according to expanded parameters the *Knowledge Book* may be considered alive, a living entity in the form of a book, it makes us think in new terms what being alive means. It also provides new information, explanations, and contexts for: Light, Consciousness, Human Beings, Computers, Knowledge, and many other important concepts.

PHOTOS MADE BY P.I.P. TECHNIQUE, REVEAL THAT
THE KNOWLEDGE BOOK BEHAVES AS A LIVING BEING.
The book:

- continuously changes its aura, as Time energy flows through it

- adjusts its energy intensity, according to the capacity of each reader

- refreshes the meaning of its text, by the cosmic energy loaded on its letter frequencies with each passing moment

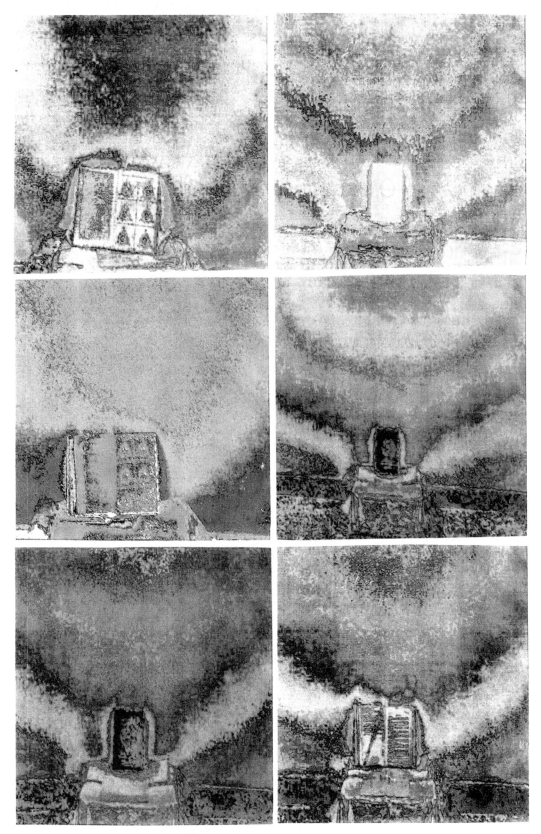

The *Knowledge Book* is an energy totality through which the *System*[5] projects its operational order. The cosmic techniques used in the book are still unknown to the world. Hence evaluations of the *Knowledge Book*, coming from the terrestrial paradigms, are inadequate at present to grasp the core of the book. However, one day our scientists will take this book under serious consideration, and with the application of their methodology and advanced technology they will come up with a thorough explanation of how the *Knowledge Book* works. Until then and even afterwards, we will be attracted to it primarily by our Essence that transcends the need for rational explanations – yet feels confident in what it undertakes.

Certainly, unless we read this book and follow its programmes, we will never know how effectively it can help us to evolve. So my deepest wish is that this writing inspires you to give the *Knowledge Book* a chance to work with you in this lifetime.

OMEGA BOOK

The sacred books of the Lord convey energies of up to the 18th *evolutionary dimension*[6]. The *Knowledge Book* is the latest celestial guide for the planet Earth, sent to us by the command of the Lord. However, this time, His direct book is conveyed through the energy from beyond the Religious dimension.

The *Knowledge Book* has been bestowed to free humanity from ego, individualism, and various conditionings, so that existential truths are able to be grasped and a necessary energy potential created on Earth. This potential will secure a future of global peace and happiness, and is essential for human integration processes which even surpass the level of our planet.

The book was dictated from the 19th dimension, also called the *Omega dimension*[7]. However, the *Knowledge Book* is a book of infinite dimensions due to the special cosmic techniques that work through it. In the future, it will reflect on us the much more intensive energy of those coming time segments.

Why has this dimension communicated with the planet Earth now by dictating the *Knowledge Book* to us? What follows is an attempt to answer that question, and to describe what makes the *Knowledge Book* both a unique and indispensable friend of each human being.

Metamorphosis through the Omega Dimension is entirely based on information given in the *Knowledge Book*, and presents my own comprehension and experiences related to the *Knowledge Book*.

OMEGA is a focal point that reflects the layers of the Spiritual Plan and the layers of the Lordly Plan. The reflections of the Spiritual Plan develop the individual and we reach them through our thoughts, while the reflections of the Lordly Plan supervise that person and are reached by attracting the energy.

Currently, Omega reflects $4 \times 19 = 76^{th}$ energy intensity onto our planet. In the future, each of the four channels will reflect 76th energy since the planet will reach the capacity to sustain such an energy intensity ($4 \times 76 = 304^{th}$).

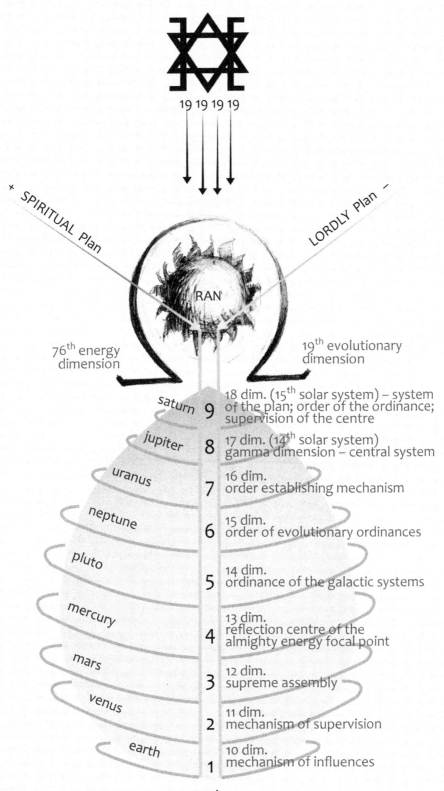

19 19 19 19

+ SPIRITUAL Plan

LORDLY Plan –

RAN

76th energy dimension

19th evolutionary dimension

saturn	9	18 dim. (15th solar system) – system of the plan; order of the ordinance; supervision of the centre
jupiter	8	17 dim. (14th solar system) gamma dimension – central system
uranus	7	16 dim. order establishing mechanism
neptune	6	15 dim. order of evolutionary ordinances
pluto	5	14 dim. ordinance of the galactic systems
mercury	4	13 dim. reflection centre of the almighty energy focal point
mars	3	12 dim. supreme assembly
venus	2	11 dim. mechanism of supervision
earth	1	10 dim. mechanism of influences

ranks

THE AGE WE LIVE IN

mars

In order to understand the reasons and the purpose in giving the Knowledge Book to our planet, it is essential to have a look at life and human beings on Earth in a wider than usual context – by seeing them from a cosmic rather than a terrestrial viewpoint.

LIFE ON EARTH

Earth is a natural spaceship. Our life here is a kind of school – a branch of the universal life-school.

Conscious energy, present/manifested in the material form called a *human being*, goes through an evolution in the medium of Godly and Spiritual energies in this school. It is heading towards the Universal dimensions and the *Dimensions of Truth*[8].

The energetic dynamism of the universe continuously reflects on our planet, providing the necessary energy/information for our curriculum here on Earth. In this school, we learn truth and attain consciousness through experience (which we call *destiny*).

All the events we have been through, including our present and future experiences, are arranged for us to learn necessary lessons in order to expand our *awareness*[9] and consciousness so that we can complete our evolution.

EVOLUTION AND ITS NECESSITY

Truths have been engrafted in our genes. The unveiling of all this information depends upon the evolution and consciousness of the person in question. Thus, in order to realise their full genetic potential, humans are exposed to education and evolution.

Evolution is necessary for our **thought, consciousness** and **cellular potential** – though not for the *Spirit*[10]. Spirit is an indivisible totality outside *our body*[11]. We are connected to it by our Consciousness energy via what is referred to as a *silver cord*[12].

The material energy of our current body is deprived of its Spiritual Essence, thus we presently live in an incomplete, ephemeral, body.

Spiritual energy is an everlasting almighty energy. It is also a neutral potential that neither grows nor disappears. We approach it gradually. Evolution is a programme which brings us closer to this mighty energy.

Through evolution, our potential on the material level thrives, aiming to match our potential on the Spiritual level. When these two potentials equalise, our biological crude mater form can claim all its neutral potential from the power layers within the Spiritual Totality that belongs to it. Ultimately, the entire cellular potential of our crude matter form will be reinforced with the Spiritual energies.

By merging with its Spiritual Essence, our physical body reaches its full life power and eventually becomes real. Having gained absolute mastery of our immortal body, and having also transformed all our cells into cell-brains, we can move through dimensional mediums stronger than the one on Earth. According to the standard of the Creator, from this very stage we are considered *perfect* or *genuine human beings*.

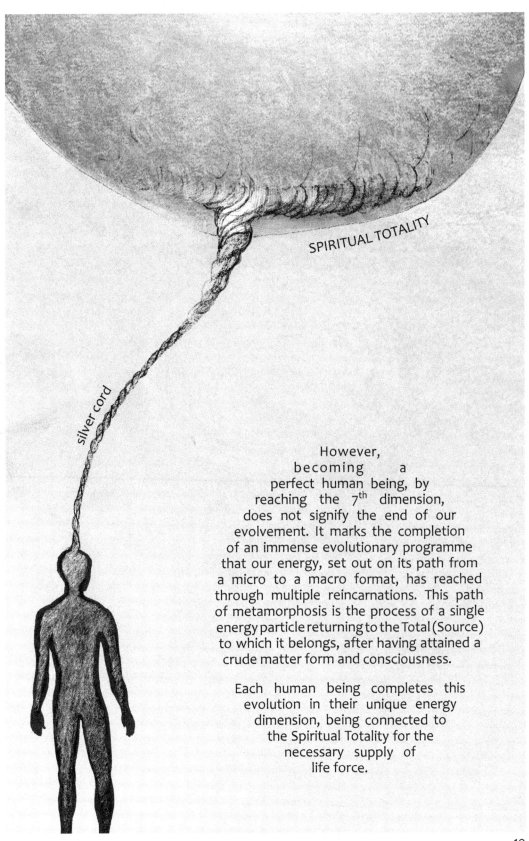

SPIRITUAL TOTALITY

silver cord

However,
becoming   a
perfect human being, by
reaching the 7th dimension,
does not signify the end of our
evolvement. It marks the completion
of an immense evolutionary programme
that our energy, set out on its path from
a micro to a macro format, has reached
through multiple reincarnations. This path
of metamorphosis is the process of a single
energy particle returning to the Total (Source)
to which it belongs, after having attained a
crude matter form and consciousness.

Each human being completes this
evolution in their unique energy
dimension, being connected to
the Spiritual Totality for the
necessary supply of
life force.

Will of the Total — All-Merciful

universal ordinance

universal laws

ACCEPTING THE WILL
OF THE TOTAL

The presence of the Creator's particle in us drives us back to Him – to our full genetic potential. It is the source of will in us that longs to reflect the *Will of the Total*[13]. From one lifetime to another, we learn to use our *individual will*[14] by navigating it towards the Will of the Total.

When we consciously surrender to the Will of the Total, it means we have understood the Universal Laws and the sole purpose of our existence. From then on, we see no greater privilege than consciously serving the Total, since supporting the order of the Total means supporting the primary needs of any individual within it. This maturity signifies the birth of *mission-consciousness* in us.

Accepting the Will of the Total permits an effortless flow of the universal power to circulate through us. This means we are energetically ready to take that intense universal energy into our material cellular structure, thought and consciousness. Only then do we start to exist in unity with all of Creation.

ALPHA-entrance – OMEGA-exit

Human beings on our planet start their evolution in the 3rd dimension. This stage is symbolically called the *entrance through the ALPHA gate*, because of the initial education being carried out through the ALPHA energies. Those who successfully pass all their exams in this life school on Earth, and building upon the foundation of the Alpha energy manage to attract and assimilate the necessary BETA energies coming from the OMEGA dimension, obtain permission to exit through the OMEGA gate. Thus, human evolution on this planet is an application of the ALPHA-entrance – OMEGA-exit programme hinted at by religious text with: *I am Alpha and the Omega, says the Lord God.*

However, evolvement has no end. Consciousness is continuously challenged to transcend the dimension in which it resides, thus evolving towards the Infinite Consciousness.

Human beings acquire consciousness in proportion to their ability to reach the particles of God's eternal Consciousness Totality.

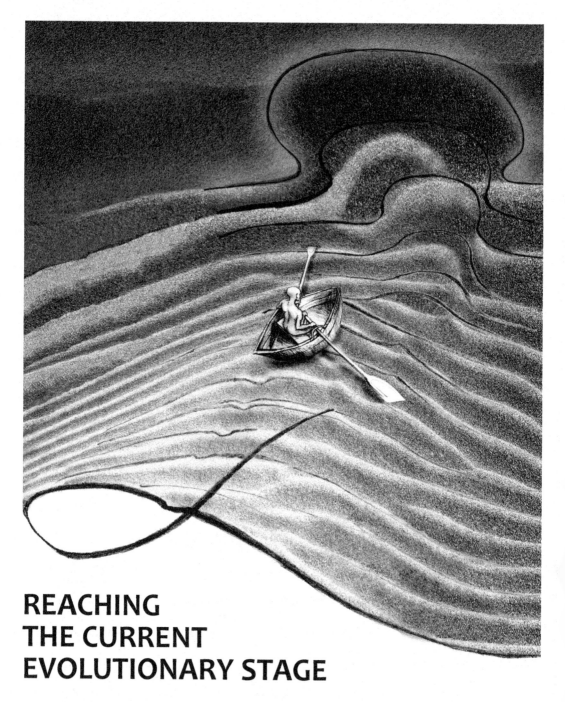

REACHING
THE CURRENT
EVOLUTIONARY STAGE

During the last 6000 years, our planet has been taken into a specific preparatory programme of consciousness progress. Within this time, the *Divine Plan*[15] started to address human beings on Earth through the sacred books and the vocabulary of faith.

The aim of the sacred books (the *Far East Philosophies*, *Psalms of David*, *Old* and *New Testaments*, and *Koran*) was to facilitate human's evolution through the energies of the dimensions these books originate from. Thus each of these books was purifying, educating and training us with its specific energy range. Consequently, they caused an expansion of consciousness and the development of the awareness of the One God.

Why is it that only the books from the Lord are the real catalysts of human evolution? The reason is in the powers unknown to us that work through those celestial texts. They have the capacity to alter our atomic structure as well as our Spiritual properties. Some of those powers are present in certain colours of the rainbow. However, their occurrence in Earth's atmosphere does not provide a fast enough evolution of our cellular structure and consciousness. Hence, the sacred books were bestowed on our planet to speed up our evolvement. On the collective level, the aim of the sacred books was to gather the largest possible number of people on the same coordinate. In this regard, religions have achieved a great success.

Purification of the human being means acquiring noble (inner) qualities such as faith, allegiance, forgiveness, inner peace, unconditional love, gratitude, altruism, sincerity, humbleness, patience, tolerance, acceptance and goodwill. Genuine human beings emanate these virtues from their Essence, not from their tongue or the frequencies of their body. A genuine human being is one who loves even without being loved, who gives without receiving, who embraces their "enemy" and shares food with them.

Amongst other objectives, the sacred books were presented to humanity in order to introduce us to ourselves, and to prepare us for the demands of the current Age. It is always the energy of the old that brings the new into existence, and so nothing is ever lost. However, the ultimate aim of globally uniting human beings through the sacred books was not achieved. Due to misinterpretations by humanity, we failed to use these perfect books of God to fulfil their intended mission.

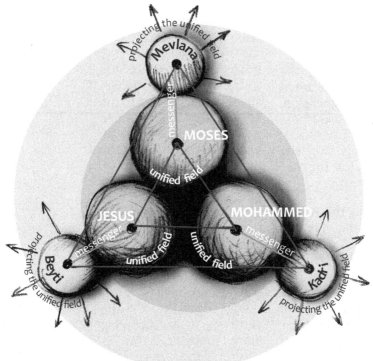

When, by the light of his/her own consciousness, a person reaches the frequency of the magnetic aura of the sacred book he/she believes in, he/she receives the protection of that unified field. This is achieved only by a loyal devotion to God. However, in order to be accepted into the protection of the System (within the aura of the Knowledge Book that is being formed), it is necessary to consciously serve God by also using the triangle Intellect-Logic-Awareness.

WHAT SACRED BOOKS HAVE IN COMMON

ALL SACRED BOOKS WERE DICTATED TO THE GREAT PROPHETS, THROUGH THE SAME DIRECT CHANNEL OF THE LORD

Even though all of the sacred books were bestowed upon humanity in the same way, through the direct channel of the Lord called the *Alpha channel*[16], they come from different dimensions and possess different frequencies. For example, the *New Testament* was prepared and dictated from the 9th *dimension*[17], while the *Koran*, which came six centuries later, was prepared in the 18th dimension. However, the *Koran* was also dictated from the 9th dimension, since the consciousness of seventh century society was not ready for the direct energy of the 18th dimension.

Information in the *Koran*, given from the 10th-18th dimensions, was ciphered. So far humanity has had nearly 14 centuries to decipher it by gaining the power to draw energy from the 18th dimension. Over time those who managed to decipher this book became spiritual leaders, and helped others to access higher dimensional energies.

EACH SACRED BOOK HAS FORMED ITS OWN MAGNETIC AURA

Each direct book of the Lord has its own aura. These auras have been formed by the mental efforts of the people who throughout centuries have been reading, studying and writing them. Hence, the people's thought emanations gathered the frequencies of these books into separate electromagnetic fields – one pertaining to each sacred book.

However, from the cosmic perspective of life on Earth, the period of the sacred books and prophets was a transitory evolutionary stage and, according to the cosmic charts, it had been expected to come to an end in the year 1999. As the world around us shows, the situation here does not entirely comply with this global evolutionary target. In mediums where religious fulfilment (saturation with the energies of the 18th dimension) has not been reached yet, religion is not losing popularity. On the contrary, it is becoming more popular. This is natural and necessary, since human beings need to complete the evolution of the Religious dimension in order to embark on evolution through the Universal dimension.

FORMALISTIC WORSHIP

In the Religious dimension, the worship of God is formalistic; it comes first from fear, and later from Essence. The worship of God required from now on is founded on Knowledge and Consciousness beyond the Religious dimension, yet it also comes from one's Essence. Those who cannot transcend fear and formalistic worship are not considered purified.

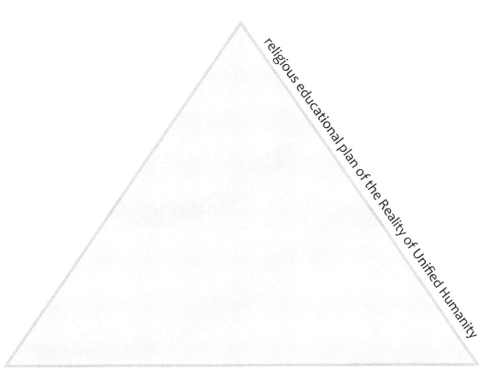

religious educational plan of the Reality of Unified Humanity

CELESTIAL BOOKS

Each sacred book is an evolutionary manual, energetically prepared to help a human to evolve through a particular frequency spectrum. They are Divine suggestions which have been preparing us through centuries for the challenges of the current age and future in the universal dimensions unknown to us.

MOVING TO MORE ADVANCED DIMENSIONS

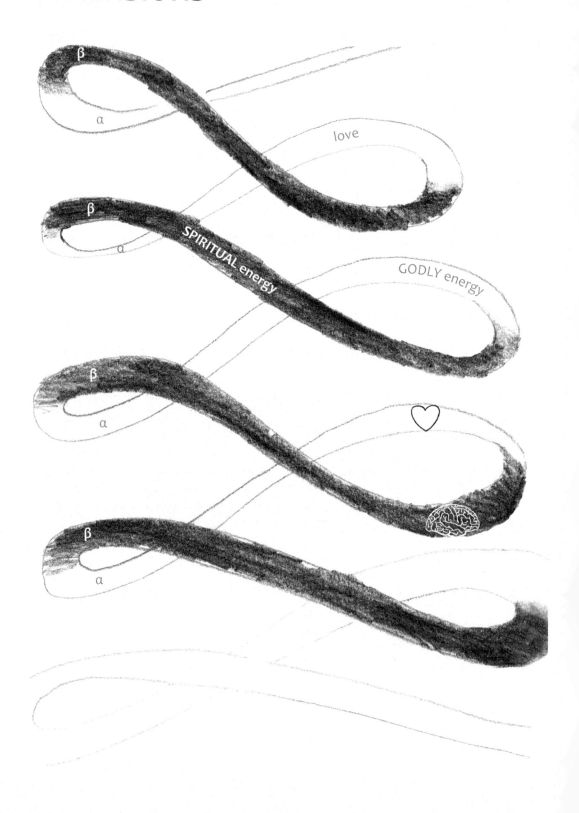

In order to move to more advanced dimensions, it has always been necessary to become accustomed to higher dimensional energies beforehand, while still on the lower evolutionary dimensions. For a human being on the 3rd dimension on Earth, evolution through the Religious dimension therefore requires the accommodation of our thoughts, consciousness and cellular potential to the energy range between the 4th and 18th dimensions – which started as a programme related to the ALPHA energies.

Alpha energies of the Religious dimension are Godly energy, and are symbolised by a white colour. We receive them through the crown chakra and reflect them. They do not stay within us. However, at our current evolutionary level, it is no longer enough to achieve religious fulfilment by saturation with Alpha energies.

We need to attract higher energies, through both our cellular and cerebral powers, to be able to graduate from this school of life on Earth. This graduation will also open to us the exit door of our natural Alpha *Gürz Crystal*[18] for the first time in human history. The right to depart from this mega living structure is gained through working in the Golden Age programme. According to that programme, after evolving through the entire energy range of our Alpha Gürz, the next destination for perfect human beings is *Beta Nova*[19] – a main nucleus-world of the future first *Beta Gürz*[20].

Millions of years ago this target had been established for energies which stepped into existence in order to reach the level of a genuine human being. As personified evolving energy that is going through its final tests as a human, we are incarnated on Earth now, since our planet is both the entrance and the exit gate of evolution within our entire Gürz. The new energies we need for this grand finale are BETA energies from the 19th dimension – Omega.

Beta energies are symbolised by a black colour. They are Spiritual energies, beyond Godly energies, and we need to accumulate them in our bones. However, as we evolve through all nine Beta energy layers of the Omega dimension, only the energy of the first six layers is reflected onto our environment by our cellular functions. The energy of the seventh and eighth layers, we keep for ourselves. This means that the energy of these two layers cannot be reflected onto us. We have to attract them by our own powers – even a mother cannot do it for her child! The ninth layer is the conveying layer.

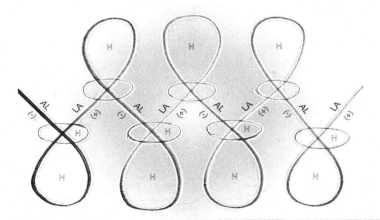

SPIRAL VIBRATIONS are "LA" frequency of the Musical Universe (Altona)
(435 Hz on our planet; colour – violet)
At the point where the "AL" and "LA" frequencies meet,
the Existential dimension is formed

GETTING BETA ENERGIES

To assist us in this evolutionary task, from the year 1900 Earth has become the subject of accelerated evolution, according to the decision of the Divine Plan and the direct command of the Lord. Hence, special cosmic currents have been directed to our planet.

In order for us to be able to receive Beta energy from the Omega dimension, these currents are being sent to purify the entire planet and speed up the evolvement of people – both of their biological body and of their consciousness. So the medium for unprecedented transformation on Earth has been prepared and a cosmic awakening has begun.

The revolution in art, technology and science, which happened at the beginning of the 20th century, was caused by the inrush of these special cosmic currents. Individuals who were able to attract and process them offered new art forms and revolutionary technological inventions to this world.

These special cosmic currents are evolutionary triggers in the form of energy pores that carry particular information for all life on Earth and for the planet itself. Their intensity and field of influence change according to the capacity and needs of the planet. For example, some currents develop our consciousness, some improve our tolerance and our love towards nature, while others strengthen our biological constitutions by engrafting them with a particular energy.

Even though we are all equally exposed to the cosmic energies, the power to attract and to assimilate them differs from person to person, and depends on the evolutionary level of the individual in question.

Our genuine evolvement degree and even our most hidden personality aspects are also being revealed due to these special cosmic rains. They influence the Essences of awakened humans in a positive way, while the Essences of those who are not awakened are influenced in a negative way. Consequently, on a global stage, both positive and negative mediums are getting stronger. The balance between them is subject to the Universal Law of Equilibrium.

It is the existential need of human beings on Earth to accommodate themselves to the influences of these special cosmic currents. However, some energy can also create pressure on our cellular functions and cause temporary discomfort or health problems. Through time, in the case of those who can receive and process these energies, their cells regenerate and their physical constitutions heal themselves. Such people gain a youthful appearance and possess lots of energy.

It is not easy to receive these special cosmic currents from the open sky and to sustain the process of an accelerated evolvement. Thus following the direct command of the Lord, the celestial authorities have offered us help in the form of the *Knowledge Book*. As a part of the cosmic reflection programme of Beta energy, this book is a favour to the human beings of our planet.

RESURRECTION

Our Age is called the *Transition Period* or *Resurrection*, while in the universal programme it is called the *Salvation plan*. One of the characteristics of this period is inverse proportionality – in other words, the truth is just the opposite of what we have been conditioned to.

It is our human Essence, conscience, and consciousness that are being resurrected now. Human beings are awakening by learning the truths beyond the Religious dimension, and gradually we are making a shift from the terrestrial consciousness to the Universal and Cosmic Consciousness.

Resurrection has been announced in the religious books. It is achieved by the triggering of our *brain codes*[21] by the energy of Time in the form of special cosmic currents that shower our planet. When our evolutionary level matches the energy of Time, our brain codes open – thus manifesting an expansion in awareness and consciousness.

divine waves

cosmic consciousness

The magnetic field of Earth is very strong, and it is not easy at all to get out of its whirlpool in order to transcend the terrestrial consciousness.

Planet Earth is a cosmic archive of evolutionary achievements of the mineral, plant, animal and human worlds. Everything here, even beauty and comfort, is arranged to attract us and to test our evolvement – simply because such is the programme of human life on Earth. Within it, various "toys" are given to us to obscure our path of conscious self-realisation.

For those who are in the terrestrial consciousness, the gate of Divine Light is closed. In other words, terrestrial consciousness is taking us further away from Cosmic Consciousness.

If terrestrial consciousnesses cannot attract special cosmic energies, they cannot make the necessary evolution. Furthermore, since special cosmic energies cause regeneration of our cells, those people who cannot assimilate them are in a state of self-annihilation. Consequently, they are doomed to stay in the dimensions where they are disconnected from their own Spiritual potential.

ELEMENTS OF TERRESTRIAL LIFE THAT ADD TO THE CHAOS ON EARTH

NEGATIVE THOUGHTS, WORDS & ACTIONS		FREQUENCY DIFFERENCES BETWEEN PEOPLE'S CONSCIOUSNESS LEVELS
EGO	PASSIONS	
RELIGIOUS ATTACHMENTS	TABOOS	
FEAR		
NEGATIVE THOUGHTS		
TERRESTRIAL ATTACHMENTS	INABILITY OF HUMANS TO INTEGRATE THEIR HEART AND INTELLECT[22]	
HABITS		

Ego is a powerful agent of terrestrial potential – but it is meant to be used constructively. If not, it is the biggest enemy of a human being and can interfere with the progress of our consciousness. To transcend the ego means to transcend one's own self, and to become godlike.

Under the influence of the special cosmic currents, fears and negative reactions on our planet are augmented in some consciousnesses.

Inside and outside our atmosphere, there is a magnetic screen that covers the entire planet. Negative thoughts cannot pass this magnetic barrier – they simply bounce back and return to the person who emanated them. This negative electricity reflected back suffocates that very person and, sometimes, even those around them.

Since thought-generated negative powers on our planet cannot pass beyond Earth's atmosphere, human beings are faced with the unpleasant consequences of their own negativity and a need to discipline their own thoughts.

As long as negativities exist in our thoughts, our world is destined to stay in the dimension of evolution and tests. By entertaining negative views, we actually damage our original Divine substance.

The choice between heaven and hell is in the hands of human beings. In other words, those who cannot get rid of their ego, fears, and negative thoughts, will live their own hell on Earth.

Due to a huge number of people becoming slaves to their terrestrial thoughts, who therefore cannot draw special cosmic energy and expand their consciousness according to the demands of our time, Nature on Earth is heavily affected by these currents. Thus, instead of witnessing more resurrections of consciousness, we witness more frequent natural catastrophes and an imbalance in the order of society, families, and on the individual level in various illnesses/afflictions.

Cosmic currents are negative in their nature, while nature on our planet is positive. People with negative energy are compatible with nature which is positive; therefore they are in a vicious circle here on the world.

Those who grow positive are gradually becoming saturated with everything terrestrial. They feel a growing detachment from worldly life yet they attract cosmic currents nonetheless. In some respects, these people do not need the world, yet the world needs them; for they serve other human beings and the planet by reflecting the advanced dimensional energies they are able to receive.

THE SALVATION PLAN

The Salvation plan is a 300-year period of accelerated evolution on our planet. This Plan introduced the use of special cosmic energies in a green-house manner, prepared for the salvation of all living entities on Earth. As a part of the universal unification programme, it was initiated in the year 1900.

The ultimate aim of the Salvation plan on our planet is to enable as many people as possible to complete the evolution of the Religious dimension, then of the Omega dimension, and afterwards as genuine human beings to get permission to exit the Omega dimension – according to the ALPHA-entrance – OMEGA-exit programme of human evolution on Earth. For that reason, everyone needs to be connected to the System – even those who have reached the 6th dimension, called *Nirvana*[23]. The System is the sole authority that can give permission to this particular dimensional transition.

The System is the method by which the Power named *ALLAH* projects Himself onto every Dimension (The Supreme Power understood as God, regardless of what specific name we use for It in a given culture, is a Neutral Energy beyond form and gender. Traditionally we associate It with masculine gender, though with an awareness that the all-encompassing God equally possesses feminine and gender-neutral properties.). This System is a Supreme Mechanism reflected onto our entire Gürz Crystal from the *Dimension of the All-Merciful*[24].

For the first time in human history, the existence and structure of the natural Gürz Crystal has been revealed to humanity – in the *Knowledge Book*. The natural Gürz Crystal is also called the *atomic whole*, and it contains 1800 mini atomic wholes. (Within each mini atomic whole there are 1800 *universes* and furthermore each universe is made of 18 *cosmoses*. Each cosmos contains 18,000 *realms*, and each realm is made of 236,196 *galaxies*. Our planet is situated within one of the galaxies of the first-formed mini atomic whole.)

When entities from all of the other 1799 mini atomic wholes within our Gürz Crystal reach a certain level of evolution, they come to the mini atomic whole where our planet Earth is situated, due to the fact that our mini atomic whole is the only medium of Godly energy in our entire natural Gürz. They come here in order to complete their evolement through those energies, to gain Godly Consciousness, and to receive permission to exit the Omega dimension.

Evolution through the religious books is considered *horizontal evolution*[25], while evolution through the Universal dimension is called *vertical evolution*[26]. These two evolutions are symbolised by the figure of a *cross*. The figure of a *six-pointed star*[27], made from two overlapping equilateral triangles, also represents these two evolutionary programmes on our path to becoming perfect human beings.

The One who has brought everything into existence has designed a path of evolution, and has been nurturing, guiding and supervising human beings throughout our long history by His System. He has also defined the salvation programme and consequently has now extended His helping hand to us through the *Knowledge Book*. From the Omega dimension, this book reflects Beta energy to its readers, which is necessary for our evolvement at this current stage.

The ability to attract and to absorb Beta energies from the Omega dimension is crucial for genuine salvation. In other words, for human beings, salvation means reaching the level of the perfect human being by completing the evolution of the 7th dimension. That achievement also directly depends on one's ability to grasp the universal truth.

The time frame for the completion of the Salvation Plan is narrow. It stretches only until the beginning of the 23rd century. Meanwhile the intensity of energy on Earth continues to increase dramatically. Some of this is caused by the very application of the accelerated evolution programme of the Salvation Plan, and some is the reflection of phenomena way beyond our Solar system, universe, and even Gürz Crystal.

For example, Earth is gradually entering the cosmic reflection field of vibrations from the Big Bang. Since our perception of time is affected by the speed of incoming cosmic currents, the vibrational replicas of the Big Bang not only hugely amplify the energy on the planet, they also affect time – which we perceive as rapidly speeding up.

To sustain these natural occurrences, human beings must intensify their own capacity for receiving the cosmic energy, and ultimately claim all the energies from the Spiritual dimension that belong to them. This is the evolutionary demand we are facing now in order to continue existing, in order to secure our future.

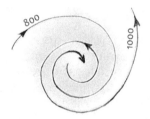

THE SELECTION PROGRAMME (1900 - 2200) – in our natural Gürz includes human entities in all the mini atomic wholes.

The mini atomic whole in which our planet is situated, is the single medium of Godly energy in our entire Gürz. For this reason, entities from other mini atomic wholes are incarnated here in order to go through the necessary exams – which will enable them to develop a Godly personality and reach the Omega exit gate.

our WORLD

our mini
atomic
whole

nucleus WORLDs
of other mini
atomic wholes

THE GOLDEN AGE AND THE PREPARATION FOR IT

The *Golden Age*[28] programme was prepared centuries ago in the universal totality, and it aims to unify all genuine human beings, not only on our planet but throughout the universe. It converges on the unity of hearts, since it reflects the Essence-desire of entities.

In order to apply this programme to our planet, the Kozmoz (*Reality Totality*[29]) has been waiting for human consciousness to reach a certain level so that truths could be disclosed to us from beyond the Religious dimension. This is happening right now with the Knowledge Book. Because of its significance to the Golden Age, the book is also called the Golden Book of the Golden Age.

Why has the Knowledge Book been bestowed to our planet? One reason is the fact that Earth is the nucleus-world of our mini atomic whole. If a medium of unity and genuine human integration cannot be achieved on our planet, then it can never happen in our mini atomic whole. This places a great cosmic responsibility upon all the human beings of Earth to follow the guidance of their Essence.

Our Essence is the first one to recognise the significance of the Lord's suggestions given in the Knowledge Book, and to realise the importance of His call to all humans to unite.

COSMIC AGES

The foundation of the Golden Age is being built on our planet by the application of three Cosmic Ages. They accelerate the transition between two radically different Lordly Orders, the Third and the Fourth ones. Each Cosmic Age lasts 100 years and in its own way facilitates the applied phase of the Salvation Plan on Earth.

The First Cosmic Age began in the year 1900, when our planet was taken into an accelerated evolution with showers of special cosmic currents. These are the energies that equally reinforce our cellular constitution and cause an increase in our knowledge and consciousness. They come from the *Mechanism of Influences*[30] to gradually prepare us for different worlds we have not known or seen until now. The First Cosmic Age spanned the 20th century.

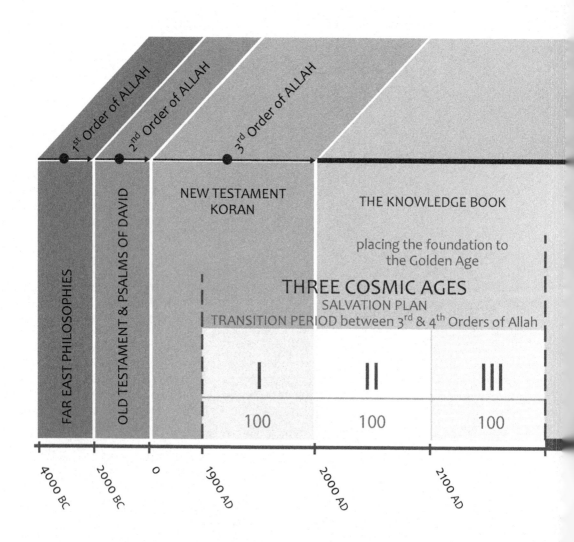

The 21st and 22nd centuries will be the Second and Third Cosmic Ages. They are also periods of accelerated transformation through the influence of special cosmic currents. Intensive exams and *selections*[31] of human beings on our world will continue during these two centuries, as well as a thorough preparation of the planet for the energy medium of the Golden Age.

Everyone goes through exams in their own thought frequency. These are the exams that test our evolutionary level by checking the presence of qualities such as responsibility, forgiveness, patience, tolerance, self-sacrifice, and acceptance – in our Essence, not in our words.

During the Second and Third Cosmic Age, the population on Earth might be heavily reduced. That is not because the Creator loves some human beings more than others.

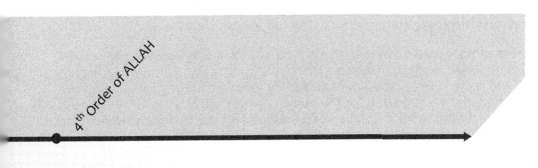

4th Order of ALLAH

THE KNOWLEDGE BOOK

GOLDEN AGE

(23rd – 30th century)

AGE OF LIGHT

(nine centuries)

3000 AD

3900 AD

It is due to purely physical reasons – the energy intensity on our planet will continue to grow, while not all humans will be able to harmonise with it by attracting the necessary cosmic energies. Because of this intensification of the energy on Earth, to have another incarnation on it would require that in this lifetime our bone cells assimilate Beta energies from the Omega dimension. It is worth stressing that the individuals who complete the programme of writing the *Knowledge Book* in their handwriting receive Beta energy in their bones.

After the 22nd century, there will be no more need for special cosmic energies to shower our planet. Selections will be over, and the Kozmoz will terminate the Programmes of Salvation, Reincarnation and Death on Earth – there is no reincarnation in the supreme realms of the advanced plans. Having acquired their real everlasting bodies of the 7th dimension, and a corresponding more advanced consciousness, in less than 200 years humans on this planet will live as an integrated whole.

Starting from the 23rd century, the future therefore belongs to those who will transcend the stage of reincarnations, and settle in their everlasting body. This body is entirely unified with the energy of its own Spiritual Essence, obtained from the universal depths to strengthen it to the full genetic capacity.

Our perfect body is also a perfect mirror of the Total. It fully receives and reflects the Total's Might and Will. To deserve that power is not easy at all. Hence, that has been, and remains to be, the aim of all our life efforts, and the goal of numerous cosmic programmes prepared for the human being. *God, May the will be yours* is a well-known leitmotif of the sacred texts, though we are only now beginning to recognise the cosmic energy operational mechanism behind it.

In the search for existential meaning, a shift of focus from Earth to the Cosmos is essential. This opens our perspective onto a wider environment, the energy flow of which makes impact on our planet and all Her dwellers, influencing their cosmic destinies.

Bringing a cosmic perspective to life on Earth makes it easier to understand the relationships between the rapid energy changes on the planet, our physical survival, and the emergence of the Golden Age. Hence, the notion of the *Salvation Plan* can be seen as being much more than a seemingly fictional religious narrative.

Upon the establishment of its foundation during the three Cosmic Ages, the Golden Age will be lived for the next seven centuries, until the 30th century. The following nine centuries will be an Age of Light. The *Knowledge Book* will also be used during the Age of Light to attract the energy of Time. After serving humanity for 19 centuries, the *Knowledge Book* will be placed in the universal archive.

In order for this future, named the Golden Age, to manifest, those members of humanity who have reached a certain level of consciousness will work in the cosmic reflection programmes related to the *Knowledge Book*. These programmes facilitate the formation of the aura of the *Knowledge Book* in the universal ordinance, and the unification of the genuine human beings both on our planet and throughout the universes. On behalf of the All-Merciful, the director of the entire natural Alpha Gürz Crystal, the Kozmoz reflects the Divine Plan within the Gürz and introduces those programmes.

ALPHA CHANNEL

The Alpha channel is a direct reflective mechanism of Allah and it is under the supervision of the *World Lord*[32]. It represents the direct energy line between Allah and the human being, thus the direct words of Allah have reached human beings only by books dictated through this channel. These are the *Far East Philosophies, Old Testament, Psalms of David, New Testament* and *Koran*. Their energy is the only energy on the planet that provides the necessary frequencies for the evolution of humanity, during the time periods assigned to each of these books.

The Alpha channel possesses spiral vibrations that destroy negativities. It is also a channel connected to the Kozmoz and is the single universal channel open to Earth. The brain power of the person who received the *Knowledge Book* is directly registered into the Centre of the Alpha channel.

The word Allah is a code, given to our planet to indicate the Power that has brought everything into existence. The true power of Allah is a Totality of Consciousness where all energies and all knowledge unite.

According to the theory of perception, Allah is a Sacred Light and Sacred Energy which acquires dimensions in accordance with the thought frequency of each person. As everyone worships their own God in their own thought dimension, there are as many gods as people contemplating God – even though God is single.

The concept of Allah has been introduced to humanity through the sacred book the *Koran*.

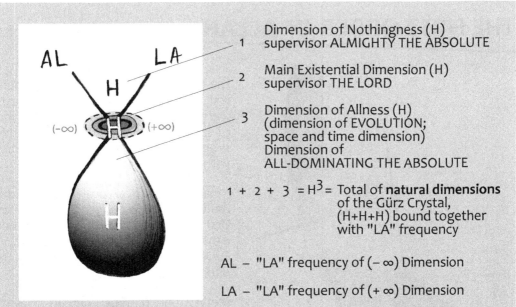

1   Dimension of Nothingness (H)
supervisor ALMIGHTY THE ABSOLUTE

2   Main Existential Dimension (H)
supervisor THE LORD

3   Dimension of Allness (H)
(dimension of EVOLUTION;
space and time dimension)
Dimension of
ALL-DOMINATING THE ABSOLUTE

$1 + 2 + 3 = H^3 =$ Total of **natural dimensions** of the Gürz Crystal, (H+H+H) bound together with "LA" frequency

AL – "LA" frequency of $(-\infty)$ Dimension

LA – "LA" frequency of $(+\infty)$ Dimension

AL + LA + H + H + H = ALLAH = Five-fold Operational Ordinance, pertaining to the projection of the "LA" frequency from the infinite positive and infinite negative universes onto two realms – the Dimension of Nothingness (1) and the Dimension of Allness (3). The focal point at which these two Dimensions meet is the Dimension of Life (2) – the main existential focal point.

From its own Universal dimension beyond the energy of the Religious dimension, the *Knowledge Book* gives a multifaceted description of Allah. It also explains the genesis, hierarchy and functions of other Supreme Powers such as the All-Truthful, Almighty The Absolute, All-Dominating The Absolute, All-Merciful, Lord, Creator, Pre-Eminent Mother, Pre-Eminent Spirit, Pre-Eminent Power, and notions such as the Atlanta dimension, Soul Seed, and the Dimension of Truth.

The direction of the Alpha channel is constant. However, over time, the geographical area of its vertical projection on Earth is shifting. Even though the *Knowledge Book* arrived through the Alpha channel, it is not a sacred book, nor is it a book to be worshipped. Instead, it is a scientific book of universal knowledge.

The sacred books have introduced the Alpha energies from the Religious dimension to us. The last sacred book, the *Koran*, encapsulates energies up to the 18th dimension. The truth in all the sacred books is offered in a mystical and partial way. On the other hand, the *Knowledge Book* comes from the level beyond religions. It is a book of explicit truth conveyed solely through the Beta energies of the Omega dimension (the 19th dimension). The *Knowledge Book* is the only Omega book on Earth.

THE FOUR ORDERS OF ALLAH

Up until the year 2000, we have lived through three *Orders of Allah*[33], each of which lasted 2000 years. The recent beginning of the new millennium marked the beginning of the *Fourth Order of Allah*[34], also called the *Golden Age*.

THE FIRST ORDER OF ALLAH

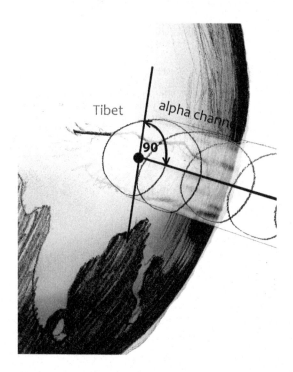

The First Order of Allah comprises the 2000 years before Moses, when, just as today, evolutionary influences were given to our planet in the form of special cosmic energy. Through this programme, our planet came in contact with Godly energy for the first time.

While the vertical projection of the Alpha channel was over Tibet, the *Far East Philosophies* manifested on our planet and the method of attracting cosmic energy by thought power came into effect as meditation.

Meditation purifies human beings and helps them achieve an inner peace. However, in order to gain consciousness, human beings need to receive knowledge. That is why the Second Order of Allah came into effect.

THE SECOND ORDER OF ALLAH

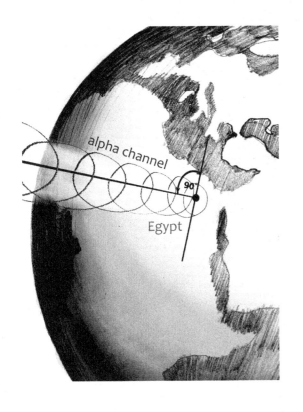

The Second Order of Allah was the programme of Moses. Since in that period the vertical projection of the Alpha channel was over Egypt, Moses was embodied in Egypt. According to his mission, with the *Old Testament*, Moses brought to our planet the essence of the ancient teachings as a direct knowledge of the Kozmoz. This Second Order of Allah lasted until the period of Jesus and Mohammed.

Only a relaxed, happy and positive human being can attract cosmic energies. During this ancient period, people went to many wars, killing each other and living through numerous stressful situations. Even though Moses was performing many miracles, generally people were unable to attract the energy of the *Old Testament* and to draw knowledge from this sacred book.

If humanity had managed to absorb the energies of the *Old Testament*, the period of Jesus and Mohammed would not have been necessary and humanity would have spared itself many struggles. The Golden Age could have been built at least two thousand years ago.

Since that was not the case, and on the basis that a human being on Earth is most happy and thrives in a medium of love, and most efficiently receives knowledge in that medium, a new evolutionary order was prepared.

THE THIRD ORDER OF ALLAH

The Third Order of Allah was a period of the joint programmes of Jesus Christ and Mohammed Mustafa.

When the Alpha channel was over Jerusalem, Jesus carried out the *programme of love* and intended to unite human beings in an awareness of a single God.

The *New Testament* conveys the frequency of love from the 9th dimension called the *Dimension of Serenity*. This dimension signifies the peak of terrestrial love that leads to Divine Love. The final stage of the evolution of love is so-called *conscious love* wherein a human being loves the entirety of Creation unconditionally – due to profound respect for the Creator.

In order to attract cosmic energy with love, it is necessary to meditate.

If those who manage to attract the energy of the 9th dimension continue to meditate, they only release stress yet do not attract energies beyond that dimension.

alpha channel

90°

Jerusalem

People very much liked the light that Jesus brought down to Earth. The first 500 years after Jesus was a semi-Golden Age, because human beings learnt to attract cosmic energy. People built many churches and considered Jesus the Son of God. Being satisfied with that progress, the Kozmoz decided to offer further evolutionary energies to our planet, and a new prophet was sent down to Earth to transmit knowledge to humanity. This is in line with the fact that for the development of our consciousness, the first step is *love* and the second is *knowledge*.

While the vertical projection of the Alpha channel in the early 7th century was over Mecca, on the Arabic Peninsula, Mohammed brought knowledge to Earth through the *Koran* and therefore completed the matrix of *love-knowledge* pertaining to the Third Order of Allah. The *Koran* was prepared with the energy of the 18th dimension, yet, in order not to agitate the human beings of that time, it was dictated from the 9th dimension.

Third Order of Allah – the vertical projection of the Alpha channel is over Jerusalem and the Arabian Peninsula

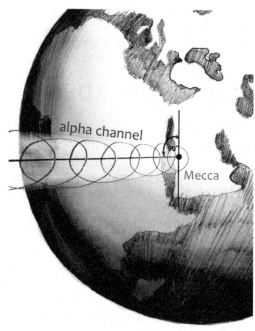

Mohammed was the final prophet, and the *Koran* was the final sacred book to be given through the Alpha channel. According to cosmic calculations made, the human being was to reach a power capable of attracting the energy of the 18th dimension in a designated time period that stretched to the year 1999. For centuries humanity has therefore been left with their sacred books to achieve religious fulfilment – in preparation for an evolution through the Universal dimension.

alpha channel

90°

Mecca

In our evolvement through the

Universal dimension that is opened to us now, we will continue to develop on three levels – the physical, the spiritual and the level of awareness:

- **PHYSICAL** – the evolvement of our body will unfold in proportion to the power of the energy we attract – according to the purity of our Essence;

- **SPIRITUAL** – this evolvement takes place through a positive modification of our personality from one incarnation to another. In this lifetime our spiritual evolvement will take place in a medium of vastly increasing energy intensities;

- **AWARENESS** – this will progress parallel to our thought frequency.

Taken together, all these evolvements potentially lead us outside the closed circle we have lived in so far, enabling the opening of infinite dimensions before us.

THE FOURTH ORDER OF ALLAH

Now, after the application of a 6000 year long programme and with the closing of the Religious dimension in the year 2000, the Kozmoz has given permission for the opening of the Universal dimension to the human beings of our planet, and for our direct contact with the *Technological dimension*[35]. What is also new is that in the evolutionary processes on Earth and in the programme of human integration, celestial assistance is now becoming transparent.

The future of our planet is on the path of learning, knowledge and science, and the Kozmoz will assist us in that direction more intensively. However, transcending the current consciousness level cannot be made by advancing solely through either scientific information or through religious teachings, because religion and learning form a whole. Only by uniting intellect with heart can we open our wings towards the Universal dimensions, whilst claiming our own Essence-Consciousness.

The early period of the Fourth Order of Allah started with the year 2000. The Fourth Order or the Golden Age is the period of the *Knowledge Book*. Since, at this moment, the vertical projection of the Alpha channel is over Anatolia, in Turkey, the *Knowledge Book* has come into effect in Turkey.

The manifestation of the Knowledge Book results from the necessary application of a celestial programme to our planet, according to the Universal Laws. This book was therefore in no way given to satisfy human terrestrial expectations.

With the use of energy beyond the Religious dimension, the *Knowledge Book* projects Universal Laws and scientific information on our planet regarding essential issues that have been puzzling the human mind – such as the origin of energy, crude matter, and the existential programme. Even though it has been dictated by the direct command of the Lord, the *Knowledge Book* is not a sacred book. It is the Universal Constitution, stamped with the seal 115-685 of the Law of Universal Legislation.

The Fourth Order of Allah is the last order in the Lord's programme of the universal unification of genuine human beings. This is an order in which our consciousness is meant to evolve through the energy of the *universal knowledge* conveyed by the *Knowledge Book*. Previously, the *Koran* brought *celestial knowledge* to the planet while the *New Testament* brought *terrestrial knowledge*.

In order to reach the 7th dimension, which marks the level of the perfect human being, it is necessary to assimilate the energy/light behind all three of these knowledge/light layers – the terrestrial, celestial and universal.

However, since in both the Christian and Islamic worlds there are people who still lack the capacity to complete the necessary evolvement through the Religious dimension on their own, at the moment on our planet the great prophets have been embodied to reflect the energies of their particular sacred books. They are here incognito to help individuals who belong to their religious groups to achieve saturation with the Alpha energy of the Religious dimension.

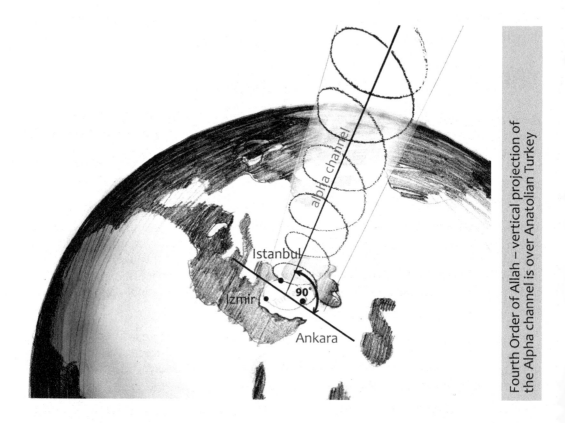

alpha channel

Istanbul

Izmir

90°

Ankara

Fourth Order of Allah – vertical projection of the Alpha channel is over Anatolian Turkey

Until we finalise our evolvement through Alpha energies, we can never enter the programme of Beta energies from the universal Omega dimension. Thus, as soon as a person completes the evolution of the Religious dimension and knocks at the door of the Salvation dimension (the first layer of the Omega dimension), the *Knowledge Book* is introduced to that person. This opens the next evolutionary stage to them.

From then on, the special cosmic techniques present in the *Knowledge Book* facilitate their evolvement through the Omega dimension, and prepare them for exiting that dimension.

The Universal ALPHA channel pierces through the Alpha magnetic field of our Gürz. As a direct channel of the Lord, it opens towards infinite dimensions.

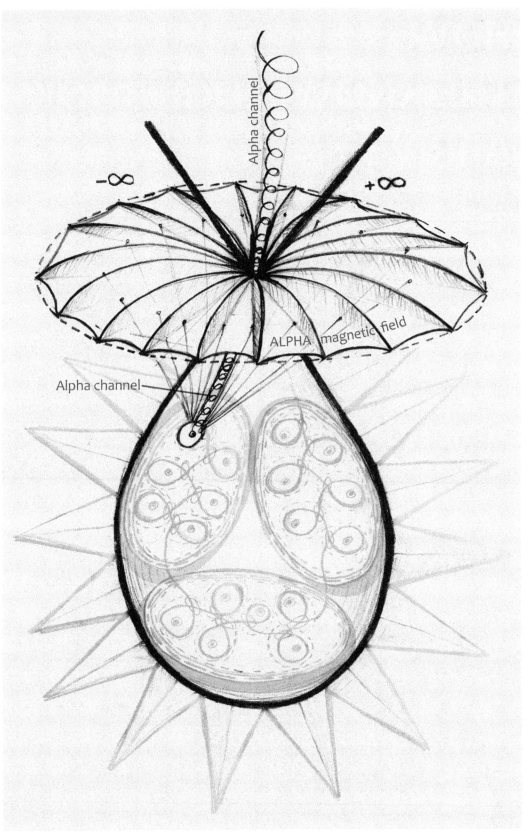

Alpha channel

$-\infty$

$+\infty$

ALPHA magnetic field

Alpha channel

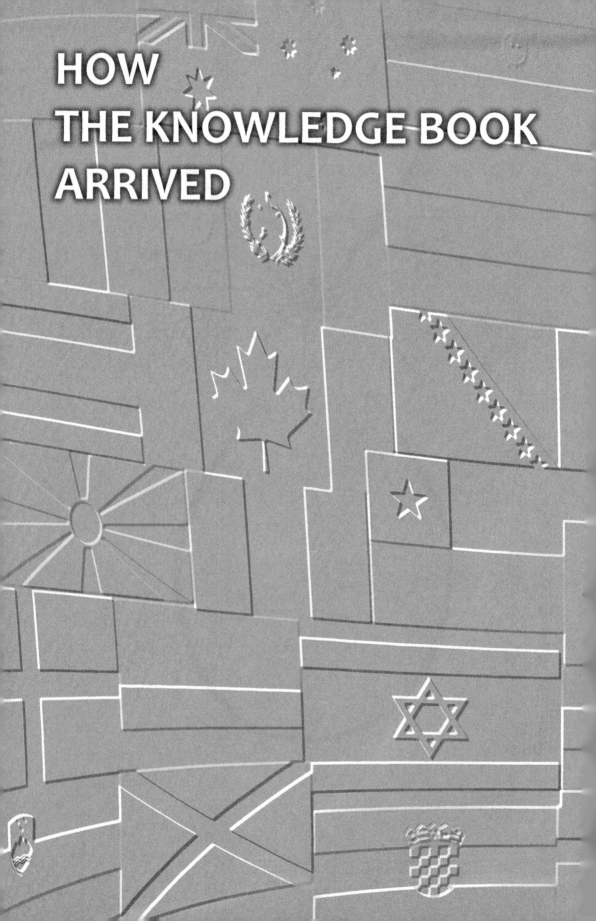

HOW
THE KNOWLEDGE BOOK
ARRIVED

The *Knowledge Book* was dictated to Vedia Bülent Önsü Çorak, who lives in Turkey. The projection of information occurred through the Alpha channel under the supervision of the World Lord. Even though the *Knowledge Book* arrived through a single channel, it is a sum of information given from numerous cosmic sources.

Mrs Çorak was born in 1923. Our universal friends call her *Mevlana*, because that is a part of her name from her previous incarnation when she lived as a Sufi mystic, poet Celaleddin-i Rumi, in the 13th century. Rumi was a messenger of the Divine Plan. His mission was to write *Mesnevi* – a book that conveyed the energy of the 18th dimension in a poetical way.

COME,
COME,
COME,

No matter who you are, do COME.
Whether a Mazdean or an atheist.

This place is not a door of repentance.
Do COME even if you have reversed
your penitence a thousand times.

Your heart is a seat of prostration.
Perform your worship there, COME.

Our embrace is open
to all our human brothers and sisters.

Mevlana Celaleddin-i Rumi

MESNEVI

Until the 13th century, in order to receive the energy of the 18th dimension, a human being needed to read the *Koran*. Some information in the *Koran* is given through the energy of the 9th dimension as open knowledge, while information delivered through the energy of the 10th-18th dimensions is ciphered. Not many people have been able to decipher it and thus unlock the full energy potential of this sacred book.

Only the original *Koran* in Arabic possesses the frequency of the 18th dimension. When translated, this necessary evolutionary frequency is no longer present.

The *Koran* was meant to educate, evolve and unite the entire population of the planet, and to prepare human beings to complete the evolution of our solar system. However, the *Koran* attracted only some people. Others adhered to different sacred books or belief groups and did not open to it. Thus, to provide access to the energy of the 18th dimension for people of all world languages, the Kozmoz collaborated with Rumi in delivering a *universal programme*[36].

The Kozmoz loaded the energy of the 18th dimension into Rumi's book *Mesnevi* by using the Photon technique for the first time on our planet. This cosmic technique provided the frequency stability of each letter, regardless of the language into which the book was translated.

For this reason, *Mesnevi*, which has been read around the world for nearly eight centuries, always carries the energy of the 18th dimension of its original, and of the *Koran*, and helps people receive the energy of that dimension.

MEVLANA

Mevlana is not a medium, nor a prophet. The *Knowledge Book* is not a science-fiction book, nor an astrology, numerology or fortune telling book; neither has it been received through Mevlana's private channel. It is the secret key of the future and the unknown.

Mevlana is a direct spokesperson of the System. In this lifetime, as a necessity of this period, she accepted the mission of becoming an intermediary, so that energies from beyond the 18th dimension could be loaded into the *Knowledge Book*. These are the Beta energies of the entire 19th dimension (Omega), conveyed in conformity with the cosmic reflection system through light photons.

From the year 1966, Mevlana has been in direct contact with supreme authorities outside our planet, and until 1980 she went on many preparatory celestial journeys. On the 1st of November 1981, the *Knowledge Book* started to be dictated through the Alpha channel.

One of Mevlana's missions in this lifetime has been to receive and publish the *Knowledge Book*, and by the year 2000 to form a reflection network to spread the energy of the book. This network was to be composed of 18 Totalities of 18 people, who study the *Knowledge Book* and apply the universal operational ordinance in Turkey. Mevlana has also established a Foundation of the morrows in Istanbul. Furthermore, being a direct representative of the System, she introduced the System to our planet.

The word Mevlana means servant of God in Turkish – the servant who sheds light on humanity. Celestial friends use this word as a symbol of the consciousness level of the perfect human being (the 7th dimension).

In the *Knowledge Book*, reincarnation is explained and illustrated by the case of Mevlana. This notion is also mentioned in the *Koran*, although without an example.

PUBLISHING AND DISTRIBUTION OF THE KNOWLEDGE BOOK

The book was completed during the 12 years (1981-1993), under the name of The *Knowledge Book*. It has 62 chapters – 55 of these are called *fascicules*, and the additional 7 are called *supplements*. The *Knowledge Book* is prepared and printed in two formats:

- The book format – hardcover purple book;
- The fascicule format – as loose A4 chapters.

FASCICULE FORMAT

(separate A4 chapters)

Due to practical reasons, the wish and the suggestion of the celestial authorities is that the *Knowledge Book* is studied in groups, and distributed within their programmes, in *fascicule format*[37].

The book format of the *Knowledge Book* was published for the first time in the year 1996 in two languages – Turkish (original), and as an English translation.

So far, the *Knowledge Book* has been translated into 15 languages: English, German, Hebrew, Albanian, Russian, Serbian, Swedish, Dutch, French, Farsi, Polish, Spanish, Italian, Portuguese and Croatian.

Publishing rights belong to the *World Brotherhood Union Mevlana Supreme Foundation*, based in Istanbul. This organisation has been registered in the universal totality as the first public and official direct focal point of the Kozmoz on our planet, and it acts as the world broadcasting centre of the Kozmoz.

From this organisation in Istanbul, branches will be opened both in Turkey and around the world. As other countries start their Totality of 18 programmes, they will grow into new direct focal points of the Kozmoz on Earth.

BOOK FORMAT

(hardcover
purple book)

THE PURPOSE AND CHARACTERISTICS OF THE KNOWLEDGE BOOK

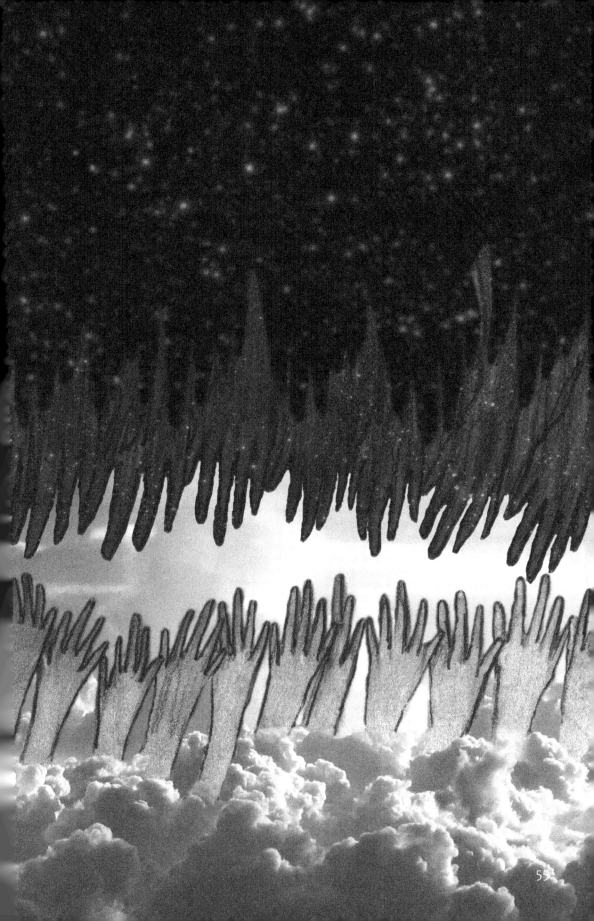

THE PURPOSE OF THE BOOK

The *Knowledge Book* is a call of the universal totality to the human beings of the World. There are a great variety of reasons for bestowing this book on our planet, and some of them are:

To declare the universal truths to our planet and to invite it into a universal unification, into a universal brotherhood of peace – based on the application of the ordinance of the Fourth Order of Allah.

To explain the truth and the life in advanced dimensions we could reach in the future, since according to the Universal Laws the time has come to receive that information/energy.

The duty of the celestial authorities before the Lord is to convey the truth to us, and our duty before ourselves and before the Lord is to learn the truth.

Interestingly, the truth in the *Knowledge Book* is to be found through numerous contradictions. Some of these are deliberately placed to test us. The others are temporarily present, due to the conceptual limits of our current levels of knowledge and consciousness.

To invite us into a medium of duty beyond individualistic consciousness, in order to form an aura of the *Knowledge Book* around our planet and in the universal totality. Individualistic actions will not be able to keep up with the tempo of the System, and so they will bring even more difficult periods to the world.

To reconcile differences in opinions and unite religions.

To convey information upon which we can gain knowledge necessary for our future – we are currently being given only 2% of the knowledge that awaits us in more advanced dimensions (this percentage mirrors our present evolutionary capacity).

To strengthen our planet by the laws of respect for human beings and for the Creator.

To assist in the evolution of humanity during this Transition Period by the power of the book's high frequencies and by the still unknown cosmic techniques that work through it.

To explain to humanity the reasons for treading the path humanity has trodden so far, by revealing relevant secrets and facts.

To guide us to exit the Omega dimension, by assisting us to transcend our own selves and to spread our wings towards the unknown horizons. Thus, the book prepares us for exiting our natural Alpha Gürz Crystal.

CHARACTERISTICS OF THE BOOK

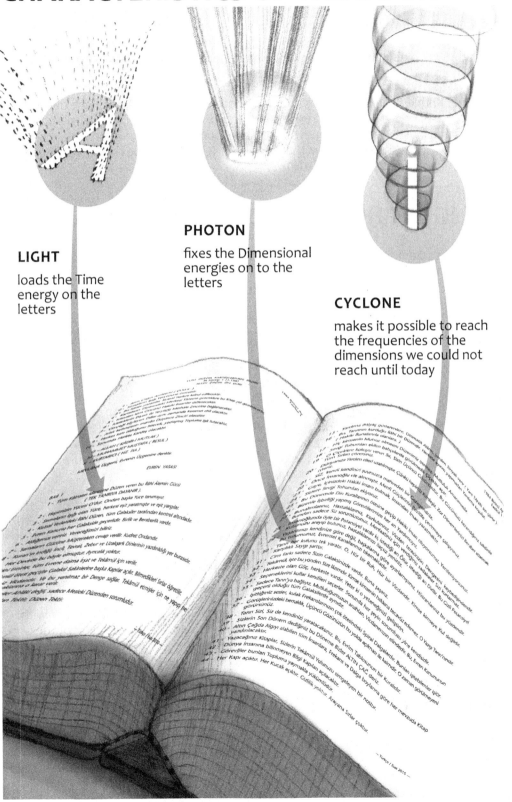

PHOTON
fixes the Dimensional
energies on to the
letters

LIGHT
loads the Time
energy on the
letters

CYCLONE
makes it possible to reach
the frequencies of the
dimensions we could not
reach until today

AN AMPLIFIED TOTAL OF FREQUENCIES

The frequencies of all five books of the Lord given through the Alpha channel so far, plus the frequency of the Almighty Energy Focal Point, as a total of 6 frequencies, have been loaded onto each letter of the *Knowledge Book* bestowed on our planet. Hence, this book is considered the single book of the Lord.

The original *Knowledge Book* was actually prepared a long ago, in ancient times. Each sacred book has conveyed to us some parts of that ancient book, appropriated to the mass consciousness level of its particular time period. Only now have we matured enough to receive information from the *Knowledge Book* in a scope beyond the Religious dimension, (and under its original title).

THE LIGHT-PHOTON-CYCLONE TECHNIQUE

The *Knowledge Book* is dictated by a technique called *Light–Photon–Cyclone*, which is unknown to modern science.

1. In this technique, the energy of Time is constantly loaded onto the frequencies of the letters and frequencies of meaning. That is one reason why, as time passes, the same sentences reveal new information. This means that when we read the *Knowledge Book*, be it now, in 10, 100 or 1000 years, the energy/knowledge of the dimension in which our planet is present at that very moment is automatically loaded on to the letters of the *Knowledge Book*.

2. The frequencies reflected on us from the book are always given in a direct proportion to our evolutionary capacity. In other words, the *Knowledge Book* tailors its frequency to every single reader at every point in time. By delivering the energy of the actual time segment only, and at an intensity suitable to the reader's level of perception, the book protects the reader from higher dimensional energies.

3. In the Light-Photon-Cyclone system of writing applied in the *Knowledge Book*, there is no influence that can affect the information delivered through a cosmic reflection system of light photons. This system converges the direct power of every frequency from the dimensions of light onto the dictated letters. Also, this technique reduces to a minimum the thinking time needed to understand what is being read.

4. Because of the fact that the energy of Time changes in each instant, the text of the book is constantly energetically refreshed, hence the book can be read every day without becoming monotonous. That way, as time progresses, a deeper meaning of the same text is accessed. Due to this unique ability to continuously actualise its own content by the new energy of Time, the *Knowledge Book* behaves like a living organism.

5. It is not possible to memorise the text of the *Knowledge Book* since the cosmic energies continuously flow through it – only a rough memory of what is read remains.

    On the other hand, we could memorise the text of any of the sacred books should we wish to do so. For example, there are numerous people, called *Hafiz*, who have learnt by heart the whole *Koran* in Arabic, even though some of them do not speak that language.

6. Thanks to the Light-Photon-Cyclone technique, the *Knowledge Book* accelerates the evolution of a person who reads it by allowing the progress that would normally occur in 1000 years to now take place in each breath of ours. From the point of view of energy, this means that our cellular and cerebral capacity has to become large enough to be able to attract and process, in each moment, the same amount of cosmic energy – that we used to attract during 1000 years in the previous Orders of evolution. Our evolvement is about gaining this power.

Due to the pressures created by the special cosmic energies, ushered in to our planet by the direct command of the Lord, our salvation is gradually becoming a question of physical survival.

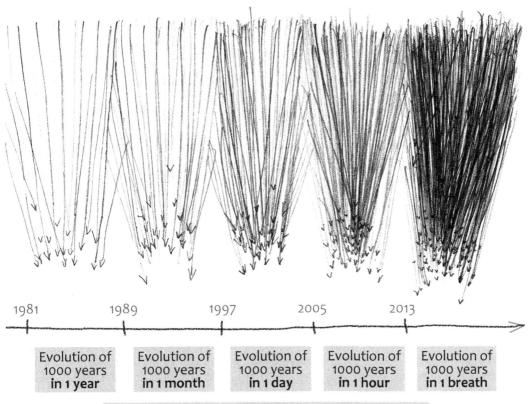

1981	1989	1997	2005	2013
Evolution of 1000 years **in 1 year**	Evolution of 1000 years **in 1 month**	Evolution of 1000 years **in 1 day**	Evolution of 1000 years **in 1 hour**	Evolution of 1000 years **in 1 breath**

Reality of our time – extremely accelerated evolution

7. The Light-Photon-Cyclone technique has the ability to neutralise radioactive energies and to alter genetic codes.

8. The frequency of the *Knowledge Book* locks everyone who reads it into their own personal dimensional energy and so protects that individual from any agitation due to the energy of higher dimensions.

In accordance with the consciousness level of that person, the book gradually opens its own energy layers through the Photon technique and accommodates that person to the energies of the 19th dimension. This cosmic technique also enables an efficient absorption of Omega energies.

9. The frequency of the book is self-regulating. It adjusts itself to the power of perception and the level of evolvement of a person. That way, those who read it receive information relevant to their own level of consciousness – without being disturbed by the entire energy of the book. This particular function is similar to the one a guru plays in relation to his disciple. However, there is a big difference: there is no guru on our planet to assist in attracting the energy of the Omega dimension.

The concept of a guru, taken as an external guide and supervisor epitomised in another more evolved human being, has been transcended. We have now reached the evolutionary stage where each one of us is to cultivate and trust our own inner guidance.

Only by facing both our strengths and weaknesses can we complete our evolution. That is why cosmic currents expose every aspect of our personality, bringing to our attention those that need polishing.

OTHER CHARACTERISTICS

1. The *Knowledge Book* is the key to our ultimate genetic potential and will unmistakably unfold it, if we work with the book and follow its suggestions. As a perfect tool coming from the Lord, it cannot fail. Only human beings can fail by not using it correctly. Our Essence is capable of recognising what this book is – a treasure trove of necessary evolutionary energy.

2. Our Age is also the period of the Last Judgement, mentioned in the sacred books. It is a culmination of the beautiful and ugly, the good and bad coexisting. During the Cosmic Ages, due to the special cosmic energy directed to the planet from the year 1900, these opposite values are becoming stronger, which has brought lots of pain and also a quicker awakening on Earth. The *Knowledge Book* declares the causes behind our suffering and, at the same time, makes a selection of the beautiful and ugly.

3. The *Knowledge Book* stimulates the operational functions of our brain. It provides a unique cerebral gymnastics in a range of Omega energies, which are new to our planet.

At this point in human evolution, it is crucial to enlarge the power of our brain. This power will grow by the efforts spent in attracting the unknown energies from the Omega dimension. Ultimately, our brain energies are to take full control over our thoughts.

4. Each chapter of the book is connected to a different dimensional frequency, and only if the whole chapter is read without interruption, does the energy of that dimension open to the reader and connect them to the protective aura of the *Knowledge Book*.

5. To humans that are depressive, this book explains the reasons for their depression and for the experienced events; it then directs them to logical thinking, helping them to relax.

6. Everyone who reads this book receives answers to the questions in their mind. The *Knowledge Book* is the only book of this kind on the planet.

7. Those who can reach the energies of the *Knowledge Book* and the Universal dimension are kept outside the programme of chaos and confusion on Earth, while they further

expand their consciousness. The *Knowledge Book* is therefore the surest guide to paths away from the chaos, confusion and negativities of the world.

8. The frequency of the *Knowledge Book* has a power to scan, to test, to train and to supervise a person who reads it. Upon receiving this comprehensive data, the Kozmoz creates ways to compensate for the evolutionary deficiencies of that person by leading them towards necessary experiences.

9. This is the book of light and the book of warning. How does it warn us?

    Here on Earth, we are not aware of the methods that the Sacred and Spiritual dimensions use to protect us from various powers. Hence we still do not give enough importance to our own evolvement and consciousness growth, and fail to exert enough effort in that direction.

    The *Knowledge Book* reveals to us that at a particular point in time, the doors of our planet will be opened to so-called *unwanted powers*, and that the universal path will be trodden only by those who are prepared for it. These are the people who are able to deal with the Beta energies of the Omega dimension, and who are taking part in universal unification programmes parallel to the suggestions of the System and the Fourth Order of Allah.

    For that reason, the *Knowledge Book* warns us by declaring truths about our past, present and future. It directs us toward common sense, acceptance of one another, and integration on all social strata. These qualities will be our ticket to universal totality.

10. To those who read the book and follow the guidance of the System, the System provides protection by taking control of all negativities in their immediate environment. The System also connects those people directly to healing channels, hence protecting their Spiritual and physical cellular forms.

11. This book facilitates an accelerated growth of consciousness. Consciousness brings a responsibility and an understanding of one's mission, which then leads to a conscious realisation of that mission.

12. Human Beings on Earth have gained an evolutionary maturity to know their future, and the archives of truth are being opened to us by the command of the Divine Plan. For the first time, the Dimension of Truth is disclosed to Earth.

    The *Book of Truth*, as the *Knowledge Book* is also called, explains the truth in all clarity to those who are ready to learn it. Those who are not ready for the truth delivered by the energies from the Omega dimension, are directed by this book to a medium of quest – since truth can only be found if one is looking for it.

    At this moment, our mission is to project the truth, warning our environment. A person who understands the truth, sees the Light of truth and possesses a consciousness that is able to elevate to the Universal dimension and to obey the Laws of the Universal Ordinance.

13. With this book, and by the application of the universal operational ordinance declared through it, our whole planet is being registered in the Omega dimension. Global work has commenced on the path of unifying all of humanity on the coordinate of that dimension – in a conscious effort to manifest the Golden Age on Earth.

WORK ON THE PATH OF
THE KNOWLEDGE BOOK

As previously mentioned, the auras of the sacred books have been formed through centuries of humanity's engagement with those books in the form of reading, writing, praying, and worshipping them.

Similarly, efforts are now being made towards creating an aura of the *Knowledge Book* around our planet and in the universal totality by studying it, reading it and copying it in handwriting – individually and in study groups. This aura of the *Knowledge Book* is always protected from negative influences.

The *Knowledge Book* can be read as any other book. However, to help humanity to evolve faster, various programmes related to the *Knowledge Book* have been rendered effective. In the name of the Dimension of the All-Merciful, the Kozmoz is authorised to introduce these programmes to our planet and to supervise their application.

The operational ordinance of these study programmes mirrors the universal operational ordinance. By working on the path of the *Knowledge Book*, we are taken into a development pertaining to the Universal dimension – both energetically and through an operational training.

With the application of the *Knowledge Book*'s programs, gradually, religious consciousness and religious paths on our planet will be left behind – but not the PATH of GOD. Consequently, a happy and peaceful world will be established and a unique world state founded on the universal order.

Each programme of the *Knowledge Book* requires goodwill, self-discipline and self-sacrifice. The friends around the planet who are joining these cosmic programmes are drawn to them by the call of their Essence. They consciously serve society by reflecting the Beta energies of the Omega dimension present in the *Knowledge Book*. The Kozmoz considers these people to be the true saviours of humanity.

The universal programmes related to the *Knowledge Book* are coded in our genes[38] and manifest as mission-consciousness. This consciousness comes into effect under the influence of the Time energy which opens our genetic codes. We are the result of a celestial reflection system that sprouts seeds in our Essence.

Programmes related to the *Knowledge Book*:

- READING – individually;

- WRITING – by copying the book in handwriting – individually or within a group study programme;

- STUDYING IN GROUPS – necessary to exit the Omega dimension (Council of 3 people; Totality of 18 people; Cosmo School of 342 people).

THE READING PROGRAMME

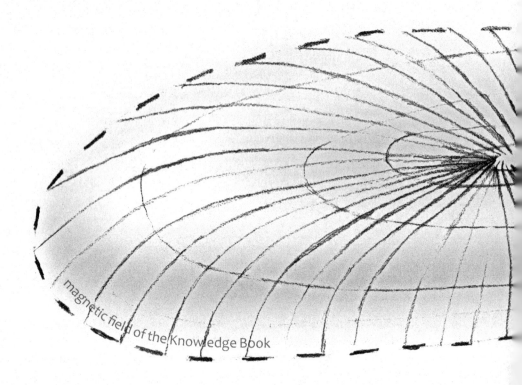

magnetic field of the Knowledge Book

Our whole planet is being dragged towards difficult living conditions due to the insufficient evolvement of the human beings who dwell on it. Consequently, the world has come to a point where it can no longer sustain negative influences, as it is already saturated with negative energies.

The urgent restorative measure for the exhausted planet and all life on it is to form a collective consciousness on a more positive basis. To help us along this path, the reading programme has been introduced. It aims to purify the magnetic aura of the planet and to neutralise negativities. The reading programme is an individual programme and has been applied to the whole planet from the 19th of February, 2000.

The reading programme involves people around the world, all reading the same chapter of the *Knowledge Book* on any given day. This creates frequency resonances of the energies of a single chapter around the globe, within a time segment of 24 hours.

ENERGETIC PROCESSES DURING THE READING PROGRAMME

As each portion of crude matter has its protective energy aura, so it is with human beings. *Human magnetic auras*[39] are formed by our positive thoughts – parallel to our evolutionary consciousness. With negative influences on Earth getting stronger every day, it is not easy to stay positive and efficiently build up our own aura.

n order to help human beings to strengthen their auras and their general powers, the Kozmoz has introduced the reading programme of the *Knowledge Book*.

All those who enter the reading programme start by reading fascicule (chapter) number 1 on the 19th of February, fascicule number 2 on the 20th of February, and so on for one year and seven days until the *Knowledge Book* is read 6 times (6x62 chapters = 372 days). Each chapter needs to be read in one go without interruption, and no chapter should be missed during those 6 reading cycles.

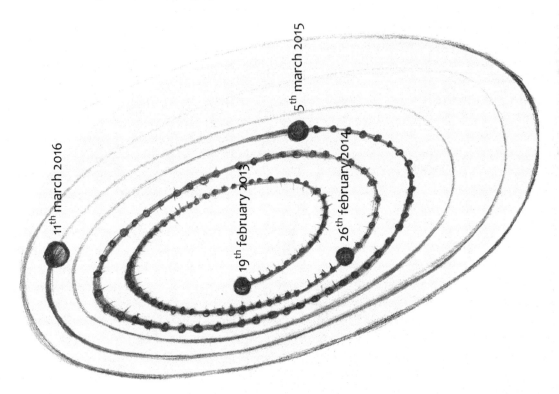

By following this reading programme every day, a person attracts to their biological constitution the entire dimensional energy of the chapter read on that day. Thus, a person strengthens their cellular structure and individual body aura with the frequency of each chapter while progressing through the book.

An aura formed this way is stronger than an aura anyone can create individually outside this programme. Even 1000 people together could not produce such a result.

During the reading programme, an energy process in the opposite direction also takes place.

The energy signature of a person who reads the *Knowledge Book* is loaded onto the letter frequencies of the *Knowledge Book* through the Light-Photon-Cyclone technique. Hence, everyone who reads this book encounters the energy of all the people who successfully finished the reading programme. This is the reason the *Knowledge Book* is called the *Book of the Human Being* or the *Book of Unification*.

Not only does the *Knowledge Book* contain the frequencies of all the sacred books, it also contains the unique frequencies of all the people who have completed the reading programme!

IMPORTANCE OF READING THE FIRST FASCICULE

The evolution of every human being, wherever they live, is registered on their private files in the form of micro-chips in the universal archives.

DÜNYA: WORLD   KARDEŞLIK: BROTHERHOOD   BIRLIĞI: UNION

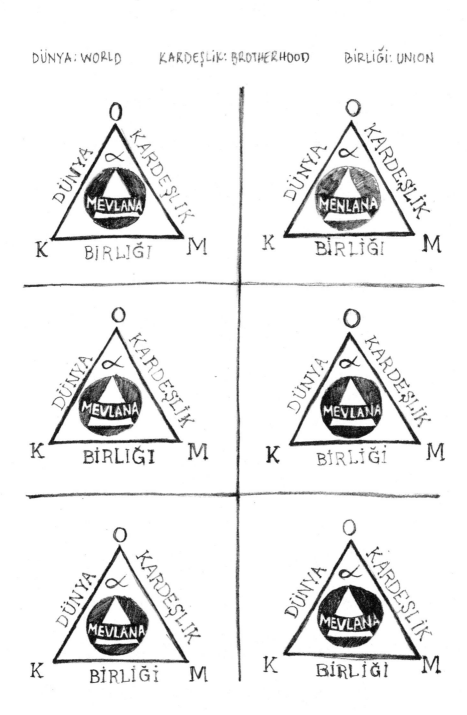

These files store all our thoughts, formed during every breath we make, during every moment of each of our lives. So, it may be the case that we forget our own thoughts. However, the universe will not – since our thoughts are stored in its archive. In the sacred books it has been said that God is closer to us than our aorta – and rightly so!

We could, therefore, assume that God knows each of our thoughts. And not only that – the moment the universal computer systems register our thoughts, the Technological dimension sends the answers to our brain. The brain decodes these signals and translates them into information meaningful to our level of consciousness.

We are also exposed to the influence of thoughts belonging to those around us, and some 3/4 of our thoughts are potentially a mere reflection of other people's thoughts. Even though we believe that our thoughts originate in our head, as a matter of fact not all of them necessarily do. So it would be better not to trust all the thoughts that we have, but rather to reflect on their nature and purpose.

Only the frequency of the *Knowledge Book* unlocks our bank of thoughts, kept on the files of the universal archive. How does it work?

Thanks to the Light-Photon-Cyclone technique, the frequency of the first fascicule of the *Knowledge Book*, as a carrier, takes the consciousness light of those who read it up to the universal archive. As a result, the personal file of the individual is opened.

When that happens, all the lives of an individual are studied. In accordance with the evolution, knowledge, spiritual culture and aspirations of the individual, their current assignments on Earth are reassessed. From this point onwards, the individual is guided to recognise the most appropriate mission in this lifetime and, consequently, to undertake it.

Reading the *Knowledge Book* widens our horizons, helps us to understand the truth, and relax. Those who cannot attract Divine waves, due to their low personal thought frequency, can never recover from depression.

THE WRITING PROGRAMME

The writing programme consists of writing the whole of the *Knowledge Book* in handwriting, in ink – using a fountain pen.

During the writing process, the Beta energies of the book are most efficiently absorbed by our bone cells, because, through a special cosmic technique, our thoughts are locked up and do not interfere with the flow of energy between the book and ourselves. However, when we read the book, our thoughts obstruct that energy flow and we receive far less energy from the book. This is the reason why the programme of writing the *Knowledge Book* in handwriting was introduced.

The writing of the *Knowledge Book* can be done within a group study programme, or individually. If it is done within the group study programme, then it needs to be completed either in 26 weeks or 62 weeks – depending on the type of group to which an individual belongs. There are no time constraints if it is done as an individual programme – writing can begin and finish at any time.

This programme started in Turkey in 1981, and lasted for 19 years, until the 18th of February 2000. For the rest of the world, who came across the book later, the individual writing programme was to be valid until the 18th of February 2013. Lately, it has been extended for the entire planet.

Those who individually write the *Knowledge Book* gain a right to one more incarnation in Anatolia, Turkey. There, they will have to work in a Cosmo School in order to get permission to exit the Omega dimension – unless they successfully work in a group study programme of the *Knowledge Book* in this lifetime.

The special favour to those who complete the writing within the study group programmes is that a certain number of family members from their gene chains are taken into salvation parallel to the evolution of the person in question.

Efforts in serving humanity on the path of the *Knowledge Book* will be rewarded by the cosmic authorities in proportion to the merits of the individual. The biggest reward is permission to exit the Omega dimension, and is merited by working in one of the group study programmes.

Individuals who have the capacity for universal evolution are taken into the Omega dimension. They are potentially on the way to completing the evolutionary programme on Earth and becoming genuine human beings. However, there is no obligation to enter the evolution of the Omega dimension. Yet each individual who steps into the evolution of that dimension is no longer a property of the world – they are obliged to serve the world in the universal programmes as a universal assistant on the planet.

Entities who do not succeed in these programmes, and who do not qualify for exiting the Omega dimension in this lifetime, will be trained in different colonies and given 3 rights. Those who fail at these 3 opportunities to conform to the Laws of Almighty The Absolute, due to their individualistic view, will be driven to the *Barzakh*[40], hence to non-existence.

STUDYING IN GROUPS

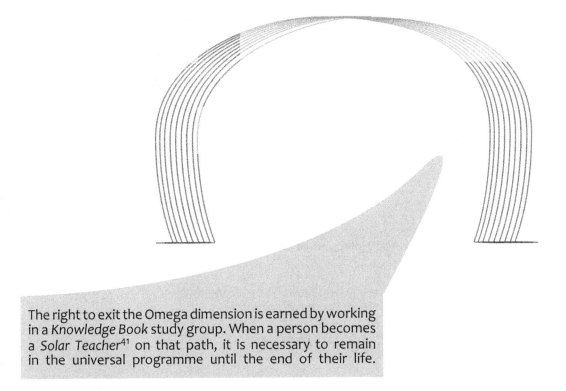

The right to exit the Omega dimension is earned by working in a *Knowledge Book* study group. When a person becomes a *Solar Teacher*[41] on that path, it is necessary to remain in the universal programme until the end of their life.

COUNCILS

The programme of Councils was introduced in 2003 for the entire planet, except in Israel and Turkey – the two countries that have different programmes on the path of the *Knowledge Book*.

A Council is a group of three people, registered into the System, who study the *Knowledge Book* following a working ordinance entirely instituted by the System.

Every Tuesday, Council members gather to read one chapter of the *Knowledge Book*, and they are obliged to write the whole book in their handwriting over 62 weeks. After 62 weeks, as a group, they open a Focal Point where every Saturday they read and study in sequence one chapter of the book for the public, while they continue to read and study the book on Tuesdays.

After the initial 62 weeks of studying and completing the writing of the *Knowledge Book* in their handwriting, each of these three people becomes a Solar Teacher. Thereafter, one of the missions of a Solar Teacher is to help those who attend the Saturday Focal Point to become Solar Teachers and open their own Councils.

Those who attend the Focal Point contribute to the cosmic reflection programme of the *Knowledge Book*'s frequencies. They receive the Beta energies of the book in a controlled, protective and comfortable manner, due to the Light-Photon-Cyclone technique and due to the study medium being directly supervised by the Kozmoz.

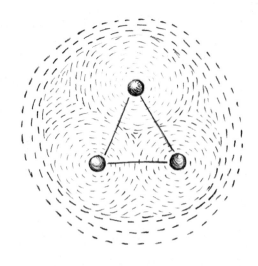

Afterwards, they reflect those energies to their surroundings wherever they go. By spreading Beta energies, they help in the mass salvation programme. That is why their mere presence in these regular Saturday studies is a form of service to humanity.

Since the year 2003, in many countries around the world *Knowledge Book* Councils started to operate. The fastest and the biggest response so far has been in the Spanish speaking countries (Inca genes). Some other countries active on the path of the *Knowledge Book* are Germany, Russia, the Netherlands, Poland, Sweden, Canada, England, Croatia, Serbia, USA, and Italy.

Councils make a horizontal reflection of the *Knowledge Book*'s Beta energies.

Each Council has to function like one brain, in order for three friends to make a reflection from the same coordinates.

TOTALITIES OF 18 PEOPLE

A group of 18 people registered in the Kozmoz for the study of the *Knowledge Book* is called a *Totality of 18*. This Totality does vertical reflection of the Beta energies present in the book. Its mission is to form the aura of the *Knowledge Book* in the universal ordinance of the Dimension of the All-Merciful.

Both the Totality of 18 and the Council are cosmic programmes prepared according to the average level of consciousness and the conditions of this period. By opening *Knowledge Book* study groups, gradually every country around the world will start applying the same plan for world unification, based on the universal operational ordinance and supervision of the Kozmoz. The Beta energies reflected through these studies help those who cannot draw cosmic currents on their own. The individuals working within the *Knowledge Book*'s programmes are pioneers in a conscious application of the cosmic programme on Earth, thus it is essential for them to follow the guidance of the System.

One of the duties of those working in the *Knowledge Book* study groups is, on one day each week, to distribute the introductory chapters of the *Knowledge Book*. The chapters given out on that day connect the person who receives them to the aura of the missionary who gave the chapters. If the receiving person has intensive *karma*[42], the karma is alleviated by the missionary connecting that person to the Intercession dimension – similar to what the great prophets of the past used to do. The Intercession dimension is the last stage of the 18th dimension and it opens to Omega (to its first layer called the *Salvation dimension*).

In order to work in either a Council or a Totality of 18, it is important to have a consciousness of acceptance and unconditional respect and love. This means that no one has the right to criticise or to reject other people, to repel them by their own terrestrial thoughts, or to act according to an individualistic consciousness.

In the Eyes of God, we are all the same – for He sees us not on the level of form or behaviour. The Eye of God is the Eye of the Essence. Being a Neutral Consciousness, God equally accepts people of all races, religions, abilities, and levels of evolution. This consciousness is concealed in our Essence. Thus by flowing to our Essence we get closer to God's Consciousness (of unconditional acceptance).

The factors that still divide human beings are their beliefs, conditionings, passions and habits. Those who have realised this are already working in the unification programmes on the planet.

Those human beings who cannot accept another person, require further inner growth. They still have an ego problem, and therefore cannot admire anyone other than their own selves.

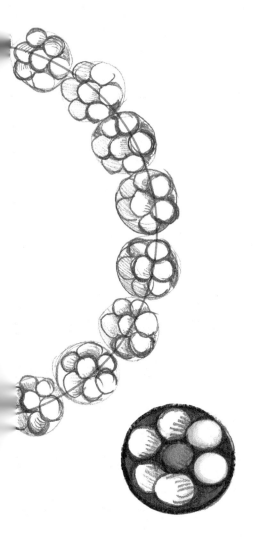

The TOTALITY of 18 programme applied on our planet is a replica of the operational ordinance of the Universal totality.
It includes 126 people (18+6x18).

In 2008, the System announced that in order to connect its own magnetic field to the Kozmoz, each country should form one Totality of 18 – and so accelerate their evolution through such an energy bridge. Turkey and Israel operate according to different cosmic programmes, still based on Totalities of 18, and they have both already established more than one of those groups.

According to the Totality of 18 programme, once 18 people are gathered and registered as a group, each one of them is obliged to write the *Knowledge Book* in their handwriting in 6 months to become a Solar Teacher. Afterwards, by finding 6 people in 6 months, each member of the Totality of 18 creates a so-called *6-petal Flower*. These 6 people in the Flower studies have to write the *Knowledge Book* in their handwriting in 6 months, in order to become Solar Teachers. Hence, ideally, 6 months after the establishment of a Flower, 6 Solar Teachers open their own Councils (2 Councils for each Flower).

After this cycle is completed, the original 18 people have another 6 months to find 6 new people and establish a new Flower-study group. That way, the Flower's cycle is repeated every 12 months. In other words, in a country that has opened a Totality of 18 programme, potentially every 12 months 108 new Solar Teachers can graduate (18x6=108), forming amongst them 36 new Councils (108/3=36).

There are already a few countries that have formed such Totalities of 18 and connected the whole magnetic field of their country to the Kozmoz. These are Germany, Spain, Netherlands, Russia, as well as Chile, Colombia, Mexico, Venezuela, and Argentina.

Israel's programme on the path of the Knowledge Book is unique. Due to the specific past of the Jewish people, their programme is connected to the achievement of world peace. For that purpose, they need to form and to maintain 6 Totalities of 18, each of which is to carry on its own Flower programme. These brothers and sisters work extremely seriously and with great self-sacrifice in circumstances often affected by war. Until such time as these 6 Totalities of 18 has graduated its own Solar Teachers (6 groups x 18 = 108), and together they open a required number of Councils, through their Flower study groups, the magnetic field over Israel will remain locked up, and the programme of world peace will not come into effect.

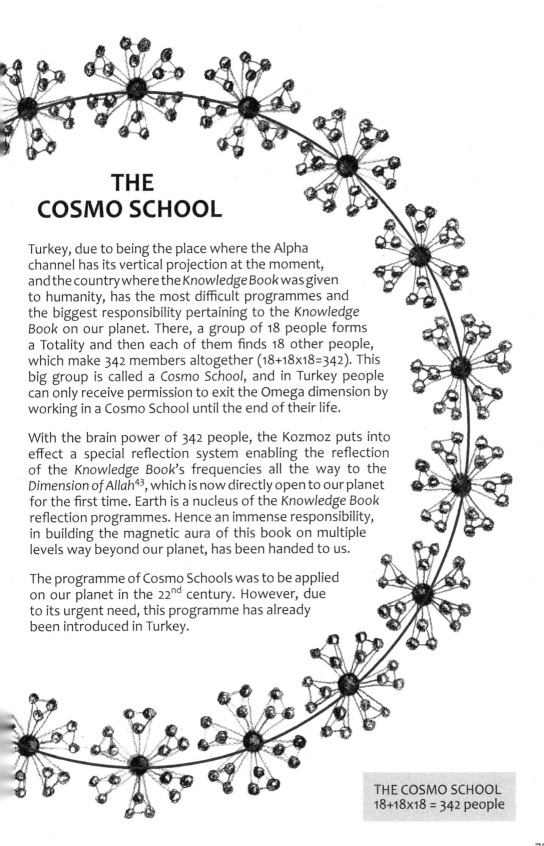

THE
COSMO SCHOOL

Turkey, due to being the place where the Alpha channel has its vertical projection at the moment, and the country where the *Knowledge Book* was given to humanity, has the most difficult programmes and the biggest responsibility pertaining to the *Knowledge Book* on our planet. There, a group of 18 people forms a Totality and then each of them finds 18 other people, which make 342 members altogether (18+18x18=342). This big group is called a *Cosmo School*, and in Turkey people can only receive permission to exit the Omega dimension by working in a Cosmo School until the end of their life.

With the brain power of 342 people, the Kozmoz puts into effect a special reflection system enabling the reflection of the *Knowledge Book*'s frequencies all the way to the *Dimension of Allah*[43], which is now directly open to our planet for the first time. Earth is a nucleus of the *Knowledge Book* reflection programmes. Hence an immense responsibility, in building the magnetic aura of this book on multiple levels way beyond our planet, has been handed to us.

The programme of Cosmo Schools was to be applied on our planet in the 22nd century. However, due to its urgent need, this programme has already been introduced in Turkey.

THE COSMO SCHOOL
18+18x18 = 342 people

ESTABLISHING A COUNTRY'S ASSOCIATION

The Totality of 18 is an energy line, a bridge, between a given country and the Kozmoz. Once established, it is meant to last throughout the entire Golden Age – which will continue until the 30th century.

When a Totality of 18 graduates a necessary number of Councils through its Flower studies, it gains the right to open a national association as a branch of the *World Brotherhood Union Mevlana Supreme Foundation* of Istanbul.

In preparation for the Golden Age, some of the aims of these associations are to support world peace and social solidarity, while spreading the *Knowledge Book* and encouraging scientific research based upon it – all leading to humanity reaching a Cosmic Consciousness and the level of the perfect human being at a faster pace.

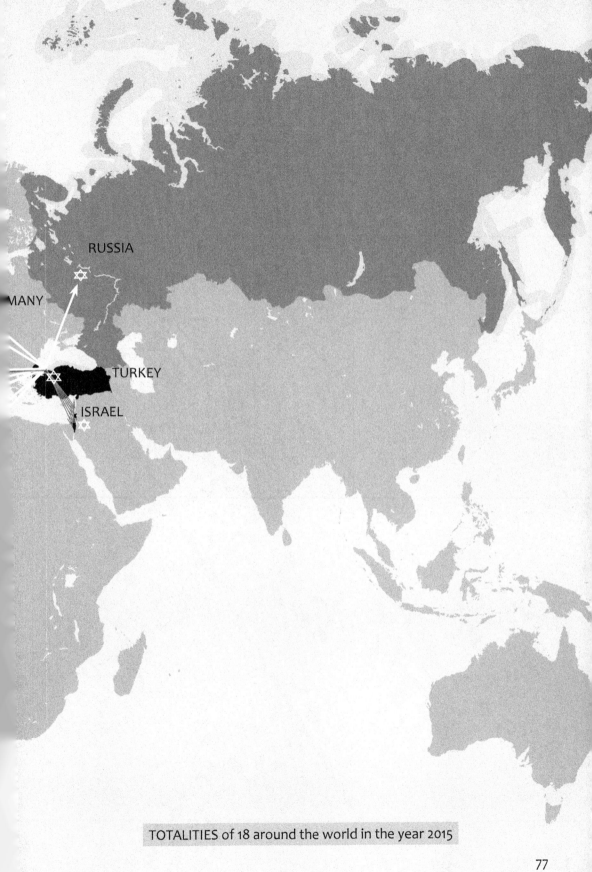

RUSSIA

MANY

TURKEY

ISRAEL

TOTALITIES of 18 around the world in the year 2015

LIVING
IN THE GOLDEN AGE

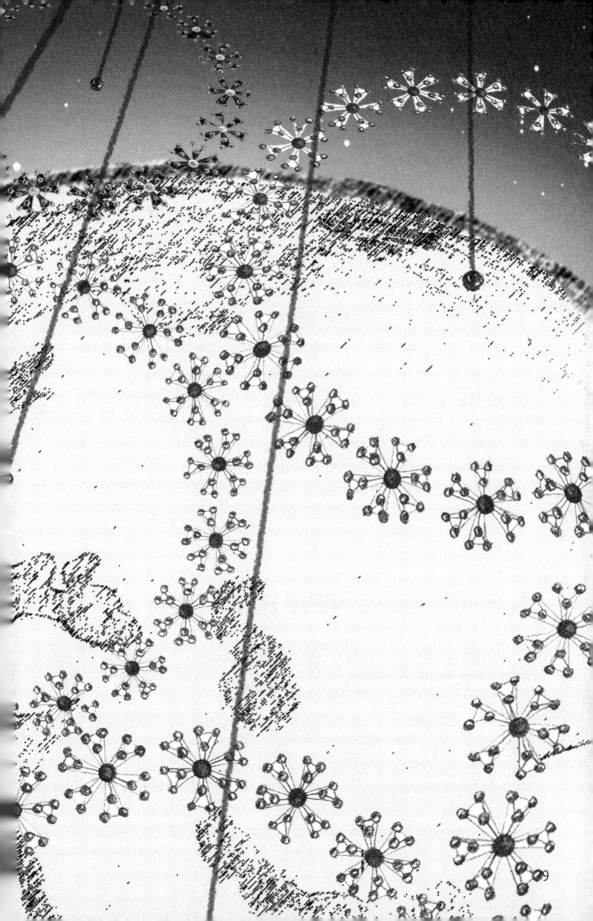

MISSION CONSCIOUSNESS

During the course of a 6000 year long period of education, through the direct books of the Lord, the whole world was taken into preparation for the *Knowledge Book* and for the Golden Age.

Many people, who had achieved saturation with the energy of religious teachings in previous lives, have been incarnated on Earth to join universal programmes related to the *Knowledge Book* and to spread its light. They are waiting to hear that the *Knowledge Book* is on the planet. What is therefore needed is to reach them, even in the remotest places on Earth, so that they can start their universal programme.

Those who already work in the universal programmes of the *Knowledge Book* have attained mission-consciousness. They have been able to receive the energy of Time, and this has activated their relevant genetic codes.

Mission-consciousness leads towards a selfless serving of others. To serve humanity is the highest honour and right human beings earn in the course of their evolution – since conscious service to humanity also means to serve the universes and the Total.

In this life, we are not here to serve ourselves, or our egos, or to prove ourselves. On the contrary, according to our own wishes and an agreement made with the celestial authorities, we have arrived on this planet to serve humanity through the programmes of the Divine Plan. We have gained our current body by accepting the challenges of that task, and the turmoil of this Transition Period.

Since our divine purpose is engrafted in our genes, no work on Earth will make us truly and lastingly happy until we discover and align with our genuine life mission of serving others.

It has always been the case that human beings have elevated towards the light only by the conscious and positive missions done for humanity on the path of God.

AN EMERGING NEW PERSONA

There are many groups around the world devoted to peace, brotherhood and love. There are also many people who are able to attract and utilise the energy of cosmic currents. However, there is no instrument on Earth to measure our evolutionary level or the amount of the cosmic energy people can assimilate.

Those who walk on the path of the *Knowledge Book*, fully following its instructions, will comfortably absorb enough energy from the Omega dimension to become perfect human beings and to graduate at this Godly school on our planet. For this reason, the path of the *Knowledge Book*, as a conscious service guided and protected by the Kozmoz, is the surest way to pass the final evolutionary exams. Hence, the *Knowledge Book* is also called the *Book of Salvation*.

Our Lord has designed a salvation path for us, so we do not need to invent one. If we follow our Essence-guidance, we will be able to recognise and precisely apply the Godly

Plan. Why precisely? Because the Lord (and the Divine Plan) knows better than us what is for our highest good and how dangerous it is not to apply His suggestions.

What happens if a person caught in a fire does not follow the instructions of a fireman exactly as they are? It really does not matter whether that person is a member of parliament, a bricklayer, a great scientist, an artist or a businessman – the life-saving instructions are the same and *obeying*[44] is essential.

For the present evolutionary stage of human beings on Earth, salvation means getting permission to enter the evolution of the 7th dimension and completing it. That permission is granted by the celestial authorities according to the criteria of the Lord.

I was Stone, I was Earth,
I became a Blade of Grass,
I became a Flower, I became an Insect,
I became an Animal, I became a Human
Being, and later I will become LIGHT.

Mevlana Celaleddin-i Rumi

If we cannot receive cosmic energy, our consciousness cannot develop and we cannot reach the higher dimensions. Biological and Spiritual progress, based on Beta energy from the Omega dimension, will reinforce our biological constitution and bring about the necessary development of our awareness and consciousness. As a result, a new persona will emerge in us. It will be the persona of the 7th dimension – the human evolutionary level compulsory for the Golden Age on Earth, from the 23rd century onwards.

GRASPING EXISTENTIAL TRUTHS

In the year 2000, we stepped into a new order of evolution – the Fourth Order of Allah, also known as the *Golden Age*. This latest Order aims at taking us into the ordinance of unification beyond religions, based on our acquisition of universal knowledge and Cosmic Consciousness. It is the Order for which the *Knowledge Book* has been sent, to declare to us the Universal Laws and truth through the energy of the Omega dimension.

The Kozmoz has globally prepared the most appropriate human medium for these early stages of the Golden Age – it has carefully seeded evolutionarily successful genes. These genes are able to learn quickly, and to deal with social turbulence and rapid energy changes. They also help humanity by attracting the special cosmic energy and reflecting it to others. Additionally, those who are in reverse transfer on Earth emanate their Essence-energy, which helps people with the same Essence-gene to evolve faster.

Our life is a gift of God. From the celestial depths we have come to this planet in order to experience particular situations and to further the metamorphosis of the energy we epitomise. However, this time now on Earth is unique – we could put a crown on all our evolutionary endeavours by reaching the level of the perfect human being. To take us there, there is a mission waiting to be recognised, the one pertaining to our cosmic origin and purpose.

If we fail to consciously activate the cosmic aspect of ourselves, we could easily be suffocated by the intensity of terrestrial affairs, by the negativities and chaos around us. In that respect, the cosmic mission offered by the *Knowledge Book* is immensely important. It can balance our terrestrial life and give it full meaning. This mission is an embryo of our Cosmic Consciousness.

Within the context of life designed on Earth, we have a freedom to determine our truth and our path – having been granted individual will. Individual will has the potential to align with the Will of the Total, since it is stimulated by the particle of the Total Will inside us.

Due to differences in human evolutionary levels, the Total Will still reflects differently in each one of us – otherwise, we would have been united on the planet already. For the same reason, the idea that human beings and their evolvement path have been designed and supervised by a Supreme Power, called the *Creator* in the sacred books, continues to be a matter of argument on Earth.

Nobody can explain what truth is to anybody else nor tell them what to do – since truth is a matter of energy compatibility between a person and the material/information in question. However, in comprehending the truth, the use of common-sense and conscience is a precious means of orientation.

Once we start grasping existential truths and laws, we are led to recognise our ultimate purpose. That in return gives us immense confidence regarding the path we walk on.

In the pursuit of happiness, every person is therefore left to find the answers to the existential questions within themselves. In that process we are both a pupil and a teacher to ourselves.

WHY AM I HERE ON THIS PLANET AND WHAT HAPPENS AFTERWARDS?

Asking questions of ourselves, investigating, doubting, reading, studying, exploring the silence, and listening to our inner voice, are all valuable means for finding our own truth – the truth that make sense equally to our heart and intellect.

Doubts are necessary until we acquire genuine faith and are therefore a normal phase in the evolvement of a person. Doubts are part of light, and are instrumental in initiating a medium of quest. Through them, we eventually discover truth and gain the Universal Consciousness. Truth can be bitter sometimes; however, its results are always precious.

Even though to some people the *Knowledge Book* may sound like science-fiction, or prophesy, what if it is not? What if the information is the plain truth, conveyed to us from higher realities due to the requirement of our evolutionary age? To consider this may be useful to those who doubt the validity of the *Knowledge Book*.

Interestingly, what we need more than information from this book is its frequency. Should we not be able to take it, we will deprive ourselves of the essential food for our evolution, and the information in the book will certainly remain meaningless to us.

We come to Earth with a veiled consciousness, and live here with a huge portion of our brain cells and DNA inactive. These dormant biological aspects are incompatible with the current planetary energy medium and are awaiting a different vibrational environment to be unlocked.

Interestingly, at the present dimensional frequency of our planet even the experience of genuine love is beyond us.

In response to this situation of an evolutionary incompleteness, and always with a bigger picture in Mind, the Lord commanded an accelerated evolution on Earth. The Salvation Plan is now being implemented, and with it the showering of our planet with the powerful unknown dimensional energies of our future goes on. These specially prepared energies of the cosmic influences are both our evolvement path and our protection path. However, the salvation of the planet also depends on our readiness to make a conscious effort in that direction, and to cooperate with the System. Our ego might not like it, but our Essence is able to accept it.

The perfect future of the Golden Age on Earth is on its way. Are we making ourselves ready for it?

OUR COSMIC DESTINY

The cosmic destiny of Earth is truly in our hands. It depends on our ability to transcend the terrestrial consciousness level and to become better human beings.

The path towards the perfect human being can only be the programme that our Creator designed for us. Should we not comply with the rules and keep up with the programme we have been placed into, we could easily be erased from it. In such a case it would be us who lose.

Whether this happens depends on our evolutionary maturity, and on the choices we make. It is therefore high time to understand our existence in its essence and take conscious responsibility for it.

The *Knowledge Book* sheds light on the origins of human beings, their past and present challenges, and future prospects. The book offers energy that is necessary for our transition into the higher dimensions, which have been waiting for the emergence of the perfect human being in us for so long.

We are to inhabit the faraway worlds of these higher dimensions. To prepare us for them, in addition to the pleasant episodes, our path through numerous reincarnations has been set with thorns and hoops of fire.

Experiencing both the fury and the grace of God is a necessary training procedure applied by the Divine Plan. If we recognise and love God only when our *prayers*[45] are answered, yet live in denial when struggle and hardships come, we have not completed the evolution of love. An incomplete evolution of love is based on self-interest – and will not open the celestial gates to us.

Each particle of the Total projects the pre-eminence of the Creator – and somewhere along our evolution we clearly reach that realisation. Thus loving everything unconditionally, purely because it is the manifestation of the Creator, signifies the maturity of heart of an individual who feels integrated within the Total.

One of the future destinations designated for such perfect human beings, beyond even our natural Gürz Crystal, is Beta Nova.

Before heading off to that specially prepared new planet, we are first to complete our homework here on Earth – we are to remember our higher purpose, to accept one another, and to unite. From that consciousness of unity and totality, and our work in the programmes of the Fourth Order of Allah, the solid foundation of the Golden Age will be built on Earth for generations to come. Such is the promise we gave to ourselves and to the Total. Thanks to the frequencies of the special cosmic rains, the echo of that cosmic covenant is reaching our Essence.

Through the Godly Essence-particle in each one of us, the Lord calls us back to our universal power. For this crowning evolutionary step, the energy of the Omega dimension has been opened to our planet.

Since the conception of the Human Being, the Total has been working on expressing itself fully through us. Hence it has been guiding Human Beings to learn and know the ultimate truths about who we are, and how we can claim our genetic legacy by ascending through the energy dimensions.

To our conditioned thought patterns, the time of our ultimate evolutionary completion might still seem distant, yet to our Essence that time might be NOW.

ENDNOTES

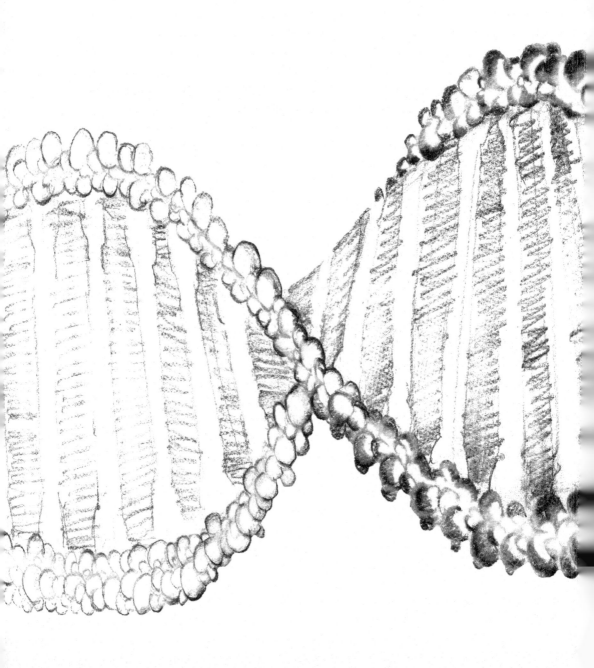

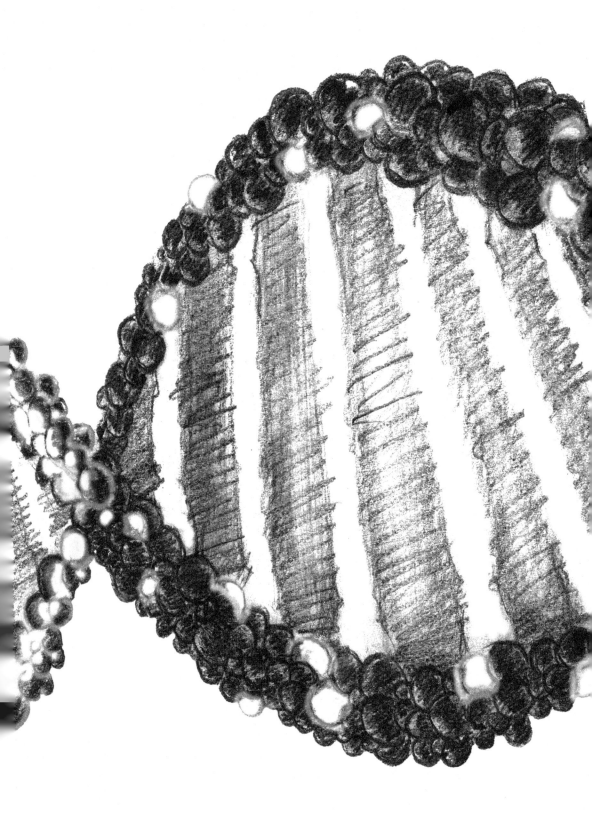

1. **Essence** – is a power potential which carries our existential programme on Earth in accordance with our gene-cipher. Due to this potential, the evolvement of Spiritual values in the medium of matter happens, in a process known as the *evolution of Essence*.

2. **Lord** – this notion, like others such as *God* or *Creator*, which were introduced to humanity in the sacred books, is explained in the *Knowledge Book* in the context of the formation of energy, crude matter, the existential dimension, the Gürz Crystal, and the human being. The names of those powers are often just a code standing for the operational ordinances of certain domains in which they are supreme authorities. Hence, the word *Lord* denotes the top Administrator of the Second Universe (also known as the *Main Existential dimension* of the Gürz Crystal).

3. **Level of Perfection** – the 7th evolutionary dimension; the final evolutionary boundary of humanity.

4. **Cosmic energy** – an expression used for rays that have nothing to do with natural cosmic rays. They are specially prepared to induce rapid awareness and consciousness progress, as well as an accelerated metamorphosis of our physical constitution. These cosmic energies come from the Mechanism of Influences (the 10th dimension), and from the left Dimension of the Sun.

5. **System** – is the System of Allah; the Supreme Mechanism, highest authority; a projective focal point of the Dimension of the All-Merciful that supervises all hierarchical orders and the entire Gürz System.

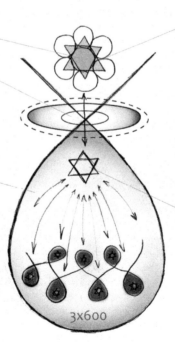

UNIVERSE OF LIGHT

SECOND UNIVERSE

(Main Existential dimension)

DIMENSION OF ALLNESS

(Dimension of Space and Time)

Evolutionary orders within the mini atomic wholes

each mini atomic whole is one Existential dimension

3x600

DIMENSION OF ALL-MERCIFUL

(its symbol – number 6)
All-Merciful is the director and supervisor of the GÜRZ SYSTEM

Symbols of the Operational Order of the GÜRZ SYSTEM

REALITY TOTALITY OF UNIFIED HUMANITY

as the focal point of the Divine Plan, it projects the evolutionary programme as two training paths: **religious** and **universal**

6. **The evolutionary dimensions** – this notion is elaborated in the *Knowledge Book* in relation to solar systems. Evolutionary dimensions represent hierarchical evolutionary stages, arranged according to the levels of consciousness. They are classified for our better understanding, even though they are an integrated whole made of energy layers of various intensities.

		Evolutionary dimensions	Energy dimensions
The Knowledge Book	(RAN) **OMEGA**	19 d	76
Koran (prepared)	KU frequency	18 d	72
		17 d	68
		16 d	64
		15 d	60
		14 d	56
		13 d	52
		12 d	48
		11 d	44
New Testament; Koran (dictated)	**LORDLY DIMENSION**	9 d	36
	SPIRITUAL DIMENSION	8 d	32
	DIMENSION OF PERFECT HUMAN BEING	7 d	28
DIMENSION OF IMMORTALITY	**NIRVANA**	6 d	24
5 supreme times			
2 tranquil times	**KARENA**	5 d	20
	HEAVEN	4 d	16
human being	PLANET EARTH	3 d	12

LORDLY ORDER

KARENA preparion for dimension of immortality

89

Solar systems and their dimensions are distinguished according to frequency level (evolutionary dimensions), and according to their energy intensity level (energy dimensions). Each evolutionary dimension has its own energy intensity, or *energy dimension*. For example, the 18th evolutionary dimension corresponds to the 72nd energy dimension and belongs to the 15th solar system; while the 19th evolutionary dimension corresponds to the 76th energy dimension and belongs to the 16th solar system. Human beings on Earth start their evolution at the 3rd evolutionary dimension (12th energy dimension).

From this page onwards, evolutionary dimensions indicated by numbers will simply be written as 18th dimension, rather than 18th evolutionary dimension. Their energy dimensions and corresponding solar systems will not be stated.

7. **Omega** – the 19th evolutionary dimension (76th energy dimension); the final evolutionary limit of human beings on Earth; exit channel of terrestrial evolution. It has nine energy layers , which have been gradually opened to our planet in the period 1988-2000.

Only advanced consciousnesses are able to attract the energy from the 6th Omega layer and above. In order to attract and absorb the energy of the Omega 7th and 8th layers, in particular, it is necessary to be *relaxed* and *patient*, to possess sufficient *will power*, and adopt the *philosophy of Three Monkeys*. This philosophy assumes a full control of our behaviour, in order to maintain harmony in communication with others and our personal inner peace. It requires the termination of our automatic reactions and, instead, gaining a full control of what we Say – based upon the data collected from what we Hear and See in a given situation. These tests are very strenuous for our Ego, which has to learn to survive the circumstances which call for its utter insignificance.

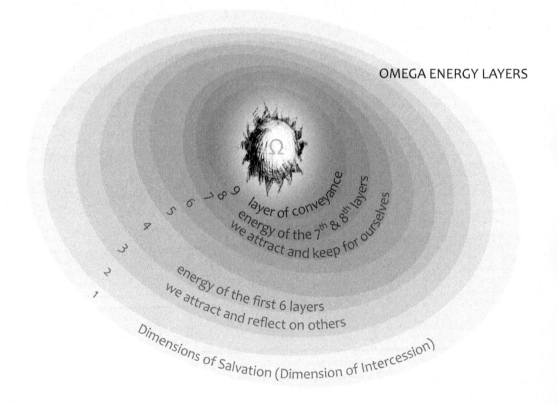

OMEGA ENERGY LAYERS

layer of conveyance
energy of the 7th & 8th layers
we attract and keep for ourselves

energy of the first 6 layers
we attract and reflect on others

Dimensions of Salvation (Dimension of Intercession)

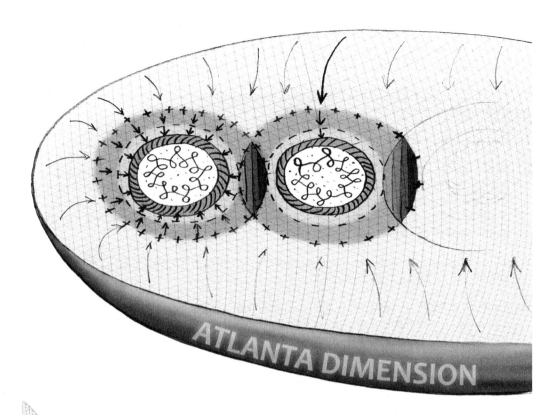

ALLAH –
TOTALITY OF CONSCIOUSNESS

DIMENSION OF TRUTH (KÜRZ)

DIMENSION OF ALLAH (O^1)

CONSCIOUSNESS OCEAN
(BIG ATOMIC WHOLE)

THOUGHT OCEAN of the
PRE-EMINENT POWER
(MAIN ATOMIC WHOLE)
supervisor
ALMIGHTY THE ABSOLUTE

8. Dimensions of Truth – also called Dimensions of the All-Truthful or Kürzes, are the dimensions within the Totality of Consciousness (Allah). They are connected in a chain of rings penetrating one inside the other.

Gürzes, or atomic wholes, float in the Thought Ocean of the Pre-Eminent Power. This Ocean floats on the Consciousness Ocean inside the Kürz.

Our planet, situated in the single natural Gürz, together with the millions of artificial Gürzes, belongs to the first Kürz. No human being originating from the Existential dimension of our Gürz has ever left our Gürz, nor reached the second Kürz. However, entities have been sent to our planet from the second Kürz.

9. **Awareness** – a state of being aware of something, ability to perceive and to feel, necessary for taking any action. There are many aspects of awareness. Terrestrial and Universal Awareness (and Consciousness) operate in quite a different way.

10. **Spirit** – Life power of crude matter; in the sacred books it is considered to be a bond of the physical body and Godly energy.

11. **Human body** – crude matter form, prepared for the evolution of energy.

12. **Silver cord** – an invisible energy cord connected to our brain that links us to the Life energy of the Spiritual Plan. Our cellular life programme is operated by the supply through this bond. Astral trips and returns to our body are also done through this cord, while the disconnection of the silver cord from our physical body marks the event we call *death*.

13. **Will of the Total** – a part of it is present in each human being as *partial will*, upon which our *individual will* thrives.

14. **Individual Will** – personal decision-making authority. Through the power of personality, individual will conveys us to the Will of the Total.

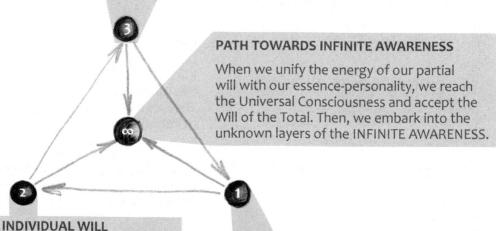

TOTAL WILL

The representative is the ALL-MERCIFUL.
This will is the universal light. We reach the Total Will energetically by going through evolution, which purifies both our body and personality.

PATH TOWARDS INFINITE AWARENESS

When we unify the energy of our partial will with our essence-personality, we reach the Universal Consciousness and accept the Will of the Total. Then, we embark into the unknown layers of the INFINITE AWARENESS.

INDIVIDUAL WILL

Will executed by the power of our essence-personality – activated on the base of the partial will.

PARTIAL WILL

Godly energy particle in ourselves which connects us with the Total Will and leads towards its energy intensity.

OPENING TOWARDS THE INFINITE AWARENESS TAKES PLACE
AFTER REACHING THE WILL OF THE TOTAL

15. **Divine Plan** – Godly System; Hierarchical Order of Lordly energies established by the Dimension of Almighty The Absolute.

16. **Alpha channel** – Essence-channel of Allah.

17. **Ninth dimension** – in the universal ordinance it is the Lordly dimension; in sacred books it is revealed as the Dimension of Serenity.

18. **Gürz** – Main Universe, a whole that contains the entire formation System of Allah. It is also called the *atomic whole*. Its shape is that of a medieval weapon – an oval-headed spiked mace – with each crystal spike being 199,500 billion kilometres long.

The first ever Gürz created (and the one in which we live now) is the only natural Gürz. It had been brought into existence after natural energy and crude matter were formed. Mankind was created in our natural Gürz, on our Earth. Our planet is both – the *nucleus-world* of our mini atomic whole and the *main nucleus-world* of our entire Gürz (see page 33).

Millions of other Gürzes, that developed subsequently, are considered artificial and are called *beads*. All Gürzes formed until now are Alpha generation Gürzes and they are connected to one another by special energy cords. This necklace-like structure floats in the Thought Ocean of Pre-Eminent Power (the supervisor of which is Almighty The Absolute), while the Thought Ocean floats on the Consciousness Ocean.

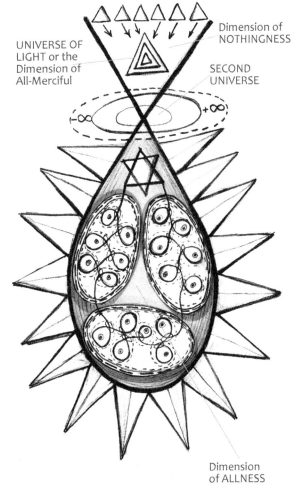

Onto this Consciousness Ocean, the Dimension of Allah (O), situated within the Dimension of Truth (Kürz), reflects the Consciousness from the Totality of Consciousness (also see 8).

Inside the Totality of Consciousness there is a seemingly endless number of Kürzes. Currently, we are going through the final stages of the training program within the first Kürz, while living in its first and only one natural Alpha Gürz.

The Totality of Consciousness is a single power focal point of Allah.

Behind this entire creation is the Golden dimension (Atlanta Civilisation), which represents the first perfect Order of Allah. Around two billion years ago, they established a branch on Earth as the underwater civilisation called *Atlantis*.

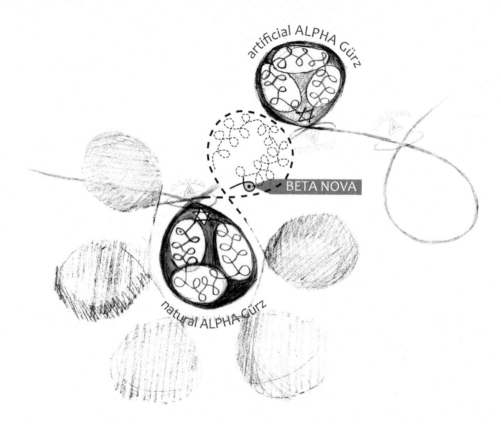

19. **Beta Nova** – a new planet formed at the start of the 20th century, as a result of energy compression between our natural Alpha Gürz and its neighbouring first artificial Alpha Gürz, within the Thought Ocean of the Pre-eminent Power. This planet has been prepared in order to gather, from our natural Alpha Gürz and from the artificial Gürzes, all those who pass the necessary evolutionary exams – and to take them to the next level of training.

Beta Nova is the nucleus-world of the first mini atomic whole of the first future Beta Gürz, designated to genuine human beings only. These processes are supervised by the System of Allah and will result in the forming of the Reality of super humans.

20. **Beta Gürz** – the atomic whole within the future Beta Nova Totality. This dimension will be composed of six Beta Gürzes in a formation of the six-petal flower.

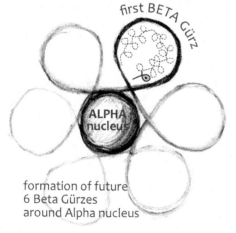

formation of future
6 Beta Gürzes
around Alpha nucleus

The Beta generation of Gürzes is not connected to the existing Alpha Gürzes, though it is also emerging in the Thought Ocean of the Pre-Eminent Power where the Alpha Gürzes are situated. Beta Gürzes will create their own communication channels and branches of their own Gürz order.

The Beta Nova Totality will carry the potential of Allah. Once completed, in its central position (surrounded by the 6 Beta-Gürzes) will be the natural Alpha Gürz reinforced with the condensed potential of millions of artificial Alpha Nova Gürzes. This is a billion-century programme aiming to re-establish the Golden dimension.

21. **The Brain** of each biological body is a universal computer. We are biological robots that are capable of discovering our own self and our Essence-Self, while serving in the ordinance of cosmoses. Once we reach a level where the power of the brain can solve secrets, we discover universes and unknown Time dimensions.

22. **Integrated human being** – the connection of the Essence-Consciousness to terrestrial logic signifies the integration of heart and intellect. From then on, the terrestrial intellect acts by the Consciousness and the voice of the Heart, and attains perfection.

23. **Nirvana** – the 6th dimension; the Dimension of Immortality and the final dimension of evolution through the *Far East Philosophies*.

24. **The Dimension of the All-Merciful** – the All-Merciful is the administrative Power of the entire Gürz; the Dimension of the All-Merciful is the totality of Central Suns situated within the Universe of Light – which is one of the three natural dimensions of each Gürz. The other two dimensions are the Main Existential dimension (also called the *Adam and Eve dimension* or *Second Universe*) and the Dimension of Allness (also called the *Dimension of Evolution*).

25. **Horizontal evolution** – religious fulfilment.

26. **Vertical evolvement** – transition from Religious to Universal Consciousness; reaching the evolution of the Reality Totality dimension and coming under the protection of its magnetic field (also see 27 and 29).

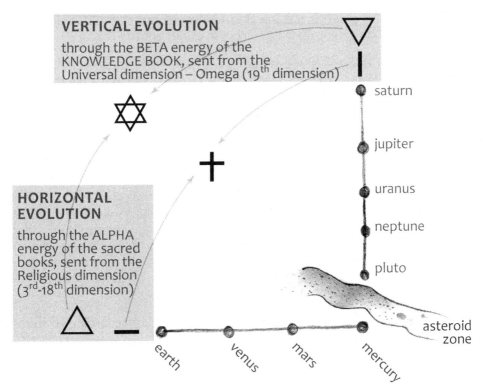

VERTICAL EVOLUTION
through the BETA energy of the KNOWLEDGE BOOK, sent from the Universal dimension – Omega (19th dimension)

saturn

jupiter

uranus

neptune

pluto

HORIZONTAL EVOLUTION
through the ALPHA energy of the sacred books, sent from the Religious dimension (3rd-18th dimension)

asteroid zone

earth

venus

mars

mercury

27. **A six-pointed star** – in the form of two overlapped equilateral triangles, represents the Focal Point of the Divine Plan within the Gürz Crystal. This Focal Point is the Reality Totality, and it is the centre where the Total reflects inside the Gürz Crystal (also see 26 and 29).

28. **The Golden Age** – Reformic Order of Allah.

29. **The Reality Totality** (Kozmoz) – is the centre of the Dimension of Unified Humanity and a reflection network of the Divine Plan. The Reality Totality is also called the *Unity of Allah*, or *ONE*. It is a focal point of the dimension which has been introducing the Lordly, Spiritual and Technological Orders to us, and was involved in conveying both the sacred books and the *Knowledge Book* to our planet. The Reality also supervises the application of the programmes along the two evolutionary lines facilitated by those books – the horizontal and the vertical (also see 26 and 27).

30. **The Mechanism of Influences** – is a projective mechanism of the Plan that orients various frequency dimensions. The cosmic influences directed towards Earth are prepared according to the evolutionary level of society and come from the 10th dimension.

31. Due to the change of the evolutionary order (the transition from the Third to the Fourth Order of Allah), the **Selection programmes** are taking place in all artificial Alpha Gürzes, not only in our natural Alpha Gürz.

    Earth is the main nucleus-world of our Gürz. It is the nucleus-world of our mini atomic whole, hence Earth is the mother of all the cosmoses/universes, and consequently of the entire natural Gürz.

    Our planet is the entrance and exit gate of human evolution in our Gürz. Thus, during the 20th-21st-22nd centuries, it is the site of extremely accelerated incarnations and of the final selection exams on the Godly path of our entire Gürz.

    Those from within artificial Alpha Gürzes who pass the tests of their mediums, will be assembled on Beta Nova together with the perfect human beings from our natural Gürz.

32. **World Lord** – Directing Power of the World dimension.

33. **Orders of Allah** – the ways of establishing unity, the ways of directing.

34. **Fourth Order of Allah** – Universal Unification programme.

35. **Technological dimension** – a hierarchical order which has been projecting the System of Allah onto the entire ordinance of cosmoses until today. In order for this dimension to be disclosed, humanity has had to reach a level of consciousness that accepts the sovereignty of God and His singleness. Since that level has been attained, the Technological dimension has received permission to explain the Universal Truth to our planet.

36. **Universal programmes** applied on Earth are necessary according to the Universal Laws. They are never restricted by the terrestrial views.

37. **The electronic format** of the book is deprived of the Light-Photon-Cyclone technique; in other words, it is devoid of evolutionary energies.

38. **Gene ciphers** – each gene is a mini computer attributed with a specific universal programme.

39. **Human magnetic aura** – a net of magnetic energy formed by our thought, the focal point of reflection parallel to our energy power.

40. **Barzakh** – a dimension of extremely powerful energies which will open its gate in future. It will melt and burn weak energies and the entire constitution of entities, leaving not even a trace of their existence. Only Spiritual energies can sustain transition through the Barzakh energies – hence our need to claim our Essence-power and unite our physical body with the Spiritual energy from the Spiritual Plan (to reach the 7th dimension). The *Knowledge Book* helps us merge with ourselves in this manner, and so it secures our existence.

41. **Solar Teacher** – a person who serves in the mission of the Reality Totality (Kozmoz).

42. **Karma** – is a sub-awareness impulse which leads a person to continuously repeat events, due to a failure to learn lessons from them. In order to become a perfect human being, all karmas need to be cleared.

43. **Dimension of Allah** – the Administrative Power of the Kürz (the Dimension of Truth; Natural Totality).

44. **Laws of Rules and Obedience** – according to the direct God's commands, throughout millennia, celestial authorities have been making efforts to awaken the genuine human being in us – the one who will respect the Laws of the Universal Ordinance and serve them. Hence the programme of sacred books worked on disciplining human beings while imparting Godly rules to them.

    Nowadays, the Universal Laws and Path are revealed through the *Knowledge Book*, and the same celestial authorities are disclosing the fact that if humanity does not follow the Divine suggestions given, we will destroy ourselves. The lessons on unconditional acceptance, faith, allegiance, given through the religious texts, are not given in vain. These virtues are vibrational states crucial for human cosmic destiny.

45. **Prayers** – are keys which connect us with the energy of the dimension they come from.

I would like to express my deep gratitude to my parents for giving me their genes, their love and care; to my husband for his endless support, and to our boys, Uroš and Filip, for shining their beautiful lights on us.

My ultimate appreciation goes to Allah for ALL the experiences I have been through, and an exceptional gratitude to Him for permitting me to come across the *Knowledge Book.*

Milena

information can be obtained
ICGtesting.com
the USA
0637061117
3V00045B/74/P